Chasing LOMBARDI

The Elway-Manning Era

Rich Kurtzman

DEDICATION

ISBN-13: 978-1-62086-924-6
CPSIA Code: PRB0714A

Edited by Mike Weise
Book Design: Josh Taggert
Printed in the United States

www.mascotbooks.com

Chasing

LOMBARDI

The Elway-Manning Era

ACKNOWLEDGMENTS

Thank you, thank you, thank you.

When this project began, I saw it as one man attacking something massive and arduous. But, along the way I've received so much help, such wonderful advice and the guidance from key individuals. In short, I couldn't have done it without you. All of you. If you're named here, I truly thank you for helping me realize this life long dream in one way or another.

Mike Weise: Your editing was wonderful, but more than anything, your advice and willingness to go the extra mile, to do anything necessary was what made this book happen.

Pam Lell: Thank you for always pushing me to live my dream, Mom.

Alex Kurtzman: You've been an inspiration to me in so many ways, changing my life for the better. Thanks, bro.

Elaine Wall: Thanks for all your advice in the writing world, Elaine. You've always been a willing ear to listen to my blathering on about everything sports and writing. Your positivity helped me persevere.

Paul Swaney: If it weren't for you, who knows where I'd be. Certainly not as a published author, or as far along in my writing career. You've always been patient with me on Stadium Journey and I've loved exploring sporting venues for your site. Of course, you set me up with Naren and Mascot Books, too; thanks for everything, Paul.

Naren Aryal: Thank you for believing in the project, being willing to work with me and for your patience throughout all of this.

Jonathan Alonzo: Your help with suggesting Community Funded, helping me on that project as well as with the Kickstarter was all very valuable. Your friendship is valued.

Community Funded backers: Daniel Mager, Jake Koeling, Kevin Perkins, John, Sayre Bedinger, Stadium Journey, Lacey-Marie Barela, Justin Briscoe, Matthew, Brandon Globe, Jed Kellemeyer, Pam.

Kickstarter backers: Paul Swaney, Sara Jelly, Jason Soren, David Stephenson, Claton Miller, Jeff Myers, Ben Short, Aisha Hassine, Sporting Puma, Lloyd Rothwell, Meg Minard, Andrea Smith, Brittney Bentfield, Lou Muston, B.C. Barela.

To Andrew Mason, Vic Lombardi, Terry Frei, Benjamin Hochman, Chris Dempsey, Woody Paige, Mike Klis, Colin Daniels; thank you all for doing a great job of covering the Broncos and lending your words through twitter and published pieces to this work.

J.A Adande, Stu Scott, Keith Olbermann, and all the men above have been professional inspirations and many of you Denver writers have been kind enough to help me grow as a journalist. Thank you. To Matt Moore for being an awesome twitterer and for debating AFC West football with me on the twitteersphere.

Thank you to the litany of websites that have given me a shot to write for you over the years.

Thank you Jessica Weinberg, Peter Burns, James Merilatt, Will Peterson, Doug Ottewill, Jon Heath, Troy Dunn, Ryan Krous, Paul Kirk, Danny Mattie, Stu Buchanon, Lou Musto, Diddy, Maile, and everyone else I forgot to mention, I love you, too.

A special thank you to Patrick Smyth and the Denver Broncos for use of quotes.

CHAPTER 1

Broncos–Ravens,
January 2013, AFC Divisional Playoff Game

---///---

> *"To the winner, there is 100-percent elation, 100-percent fun, 100-percent laughter; and yet the only thing left to the loser is resolution and determination."*
>
> ~ *Vince Lombardi*

This is it.

The Denver Broncos gave everything they had during the 2012 season to be in this position. In fact, everything they did over the last two-plus years helped shape this team into a winner, in one way or another. They were after one thing. This group of men had a singular focus. Make no mistake, these warriors were "Chasing Lombardi."

The firing of iconic head coach Mike Shanahan, the only man ever to bring a Super Bowl to Denver (having done so in back-to-back seasons, 1997 & 1998), led to the hiring of Josh McDaniels. Coach McDaniels matriculated to the Broncos from New England where he was mentored by a masterful coach himself, Bill Belichick. Unfortunately, the tutoring and experience he received in the northeast didn't translate into Mile High success. McDaniels drove the team into the ground—that started it all.

This was Denver's Boston Tea Party; the revolution had begun. McDaniels ran the once-proud franchise into an iceberg and watched it sink slowly to the bottom of a bitterly frigid sea. After the bumbling young coach alienated and pushed out players like Jay Cutler and Brandon Marshall, the fans wanted blood. He was ultimately held responsible for blunder after blooper, being booted from his position quickly.

John Elway being hired to resurrect the once great franchise can be identified as the turning point—the revolution had legs. The captain of the comeback, worshiped for years in the Rocky Mountain Region, was called on to once again bring his Broncos back from the brink of disaster. The Duke of Denver proved all doubters wrong by not only succeeding in the front office, but by excelling as an aggressive executive.

The Elway—Manning era had begun.

The Broncos suddenly, seemingly had everything in their favor, thanks to Elway's steadfast leadership.

The only thing left to do was win the game. This huge, incredibly impactful playoff game could serve to punctuate the early success Elway had found with an exclamation point.

During the 2012 season, Elway's man Peyton Manning led his Broncos to a dominant 13-3 record while going a perfect 8-0 in the AFC West division; it meant a first round bye and the No. 1 seed.

It was truly incredible, really, what Manning was able to do in his first year with the team. After 15 seasons with the Indianapolis Colts, Manning was cut. After four complicated neck surgeries, his playing ability was in question. He was signed by legendary Super Bowl architect and Vice President of Football Operations, John Elway. Manning quickly implemented his offense, leaning heavily on his exacting attention to detail. It was Manning's way or the highway for teammates, and they learned quickly or felt the football god's wrath.

This is Peyton Manning we're talking about, the NFL's only five-time regular season Most Valuable Player, not to mention his status as a Super Bowl winner and MVP. Throughout his career, he led the Colts to the playoffs nearly every season, re-creating NFL offenses as we now know them today.

There is only one No. 18. He will absolutely go down as one of the greatest quarterbacks in the history of the National Football League.

While audibling was part of the game before Manning, no one ever did it in quite the way he does, nor has anyone been able to mimic his orchestrating of the offense to date. It's an incredible amount of detail for anyone to understand, let alone a youthful wide receiver corps. Eric Decker and Demaryius Thomas, who were both drafted by the Broncos in 2010 by McDaniels, struggled at times to get on the same page with their quarterback. Fortunately for fans, they found a solid mentor and fast friend in one of the greatest field-generals to ever lace up cleats and squeeze into a helmet.

Of course, it wasn't just about the receivers adjusting. It was a similar problem for the offensive line and running backs; when Manning changes the play, you better damn well know what your assignment is. The veteran gun-slinger will call you out in front of everyone—he notably did so many times to offensive linemen throughout the beginning of the 2012 season—and no professional wants a public scolding.

Manning had the right to set his expectations as high as he did. In spring 2011, with the NFL in the grips of a lockout, he was invited to the Rockies' facilities by an old college friend, first baseman Todd Helton. Nothing would be more important to his recovery than recapturing his strength and coordination; Helton offered access to world-class trainers and facilities. After an intense focus on rehabilitation, he decided to undergo his fourth and final neck surgery, a fusion procedure which took place as the 2011 season was set to begin.

In October 2013, Sally Jenkins covered Manning's recovery for the *Washington Post*. As she reported, Manning worked closely with his old offensive coordinator from Tennessee, David Cutcliffe, currently the head football coach for the Duke University Blue Devils. Peyton worked with Cutcliffe to meticulously film and review his workouts on a daily basis in order to make the incremental progress needed for a return to the game. His level of dedication and focus was herculean. Despite the leaps and bounds made during the late months of 2011 and the beginning of 2012, the Colts cut Manning on March 6. The Broncos signed him to a five-year deal before the month was out.

At the end of 2012, Manning enjoyed the greatest season ever for a Broncos quarterback, breaking many of Elway's and some of Jake Plummer's records. As his teammates adapted on the fly, they enjoyed career years as well. Decker eclipsed 1,000 yards receiving and scored 13 touchdowns while Thomas solidified himself as a legitimate No. 1 receiver with over 1,400 yards and 10 scores. On the year, only Green Bay's James Jones had more touchdowns than Decker, edging him out with 14–not to be outdone, Thomas gained the third-most yards after the catch and the fourth-most total receiving yards in the league.

After going 2-3 to start, the turning point of the season came in October on the NFL's largest stage: Monday Night Football. Down 24-0 to the Chargers in San Diego at halftime, the Broncos rallied behind Manning for a thrilling 35-point second half comeback. The Denver defense stepped up, forcing two pick-sixes to win the game in front of a national audience by a score of 35-24. While it was the classic definition of a "team-win," Peyton's second half TD passes—there were three of them—lit the torch. Certainly, it was a complete team win with the defense relentlessly pass-rushing Phillip Rivers, forcing turnovers to set up Manning and the offense. It was the first of the team's 11 straight wins to end the regular season; the Broncos bucked their competition at every turn.

Everyone in the Mile High City anticipated that the men in orange and blue would be the last team standing, bringing home their third Vince Lombardi Trophy.

With Elway at the helm, the great pursuit continued. The focus was on one thing and one thing only: "Chasing Lombardi."

But, this year, it wasn't meant to be. Like a trainer dangling a carrot in front of a race horse, the trophy remained just out of reach.

As the No. 1 seed, Manning and Co. awaited the winner of the Colts and the Baltimore Ravens. Despite his former team having a rookie quarterback in Andrew Luck, the Colts were expected to beat the old and seemingly run-down Ravens. Ray Lewis was on his last legs, infamously announcing his retirement following the season and before the Wild Card game against Indy. Ed Reed was barely hanging on and even Terrell Suggs was a senior linebacker. Lewis played as if it were his last game—much as he did for most of his career—and recorded a game-high 17 tackles, helping carry Baltimore past the Colts and into the second round.

That meant a trip to the Mile High City for the Ravens. It was a game in which the Broncos were heavily favored, seen as the clear favorite from the American Football Conference to move on and into the Super Bowl. The Ravens were thought of at the time as an old team defensively and, with Joe Flacco at the helm, too inexperienced offensively.

Never underestimate an emotionally inspired football team.

Lewis, knowing this could be his final game, was shown crying before the kickoff. He was their physical leader for his first 15 seasons, their emotional leader for at least his last two. Everyone in purple and black wanted to win that game for Ray; he was the boost the team needed to win the Super Bowl.

Baltimore brought their A-game to D-town, which was colder on this particular January day than the summit of Pike's Peak. It was windy, with a constant 8 MPH wind, gusts up to 30 and a temperature of 13 degrees at kickoff. It went down as the coldest home playoff game in Broncos history, a fact which ultimately proved unlucky for the home team. Without a doubt, the cold and whipping winds affected Manning and his ability to pass the ball with profound accuracy; the offense struggled.

In fact, the offense didn't even have to start the game as Trindon Holliday took a punt 90 yards to the house with his blazing speed. Images of Manning smiling and pumping his fist showed on the TV screen—still burned into the collective memory of Broncos fans—while the breath that blew out of his mouth crystallized in the air, putting the frigid conditions on display.

Maybe sitting on the sideline for that extended time froze the offense, or was at least detrimental to its production. It sure seemed that way.

Baltimore answered and tied the game up at seven, and then, on his second pass, Peyton proceeded to throw a pick-six to Corey Graham to give the Ravens a 14-7 lead. It was unthinkable. Manning had thrown only two interceptions to be returned for touchdowns all season, both to the Chargers. Quentin Jammer came up with a pick-six in the first game for 80 yards and Eric Weddle accomplished the same feat for 23 yards in the second contest. But, being the 15-year veteran, Manning didn't panic. Instead, he led the offense on a long, methodical drive capped off with a touchdown pass to Brandon Stokley for the 14-14 tie. A few drives later, The Sheriff went 5-5, including placing the ball right over Knowshon Moreno's shoulder on an in-and-fade for the 21-14 lead. Mile High Magic, it seemed, was still in effect.

After Denver kicker Matt Prater uncharacteristically missed a 52-yard field goal, the Ravens were set up with mouth-watering field position. Flacco took advantage of it as Torrey Smith burned venerable Champ Bailey for the second time in the game on a 32-yard touchdown. It was all tied up at 21 as the half ended.

Halftime created a moment for reflection. This was one helluva playoff game.

Holliday created another opportunity for celebration, taking the second half's opening kickoff 104 yards for another touchdown. He was simply spectacular, certainly putting a stamp on the game and likely earning his 2013 roster spot. On the Ravens next drive, Flacco fumbled the snap. With a crippled running game, though, the Broncos couldn't capitalize on the mistake and had to punt.

A short Raven drive that started deep in their own territory resulted in a punt, and after moving down field 20 yards, Manning made another mistake. On 3rd & 10, Manning dropped back and Paul Kruger ripped the ball out, forcing and then recovering the fumble to give Baltimore dominant field position.

Starting at Denver's 37, the Ravens decided to give the Broncos a heavy dose of Ray Rice. The short, strong back rushed five straight times—featuring a 32-yard scamper up the middle—finished with a one-yard touchdown plunge to tie the game at 28.

As the fourth quarter began—and nerves started to show—the two teams took turns going three-and-out.

The Broncos began at their own 12 yard-line. Manning used a lot of rookie running back Ronnie Hillman, along with his tight ends, to move the ball into and through Baltimore territory. Once down to the 17, Manning ran play-action to Hillman, only to hit Demaryius Thomas on the bubble screen. As the ball flew through the thin air to DT, right tackle Orlando Franklin and receiver Brandon Stokley locked in on blocks, controlling two would-be tacklers. Still, Thomas went inside and threw a nasty stiff-arm to Ed Reed's right shoulder, pushing the hard-hitting safety to the ground before bouncing outside to run away from a diving Ray Lewis and walk in for the score. It was 35-28, Denver. Thomas' freakish athleticism showed on that play; not only is his speed crazy-good, but his strength is straight-up silly; the 6'4" receiver is and was one of the most difficult players in the NFL to bring down. This is why the man's yards after the catch (YAC) is awe-inspiring. In 2012, he was fourth in YAC, in 2013 he was first in the NFL.

Baltimore got the ball back with 7:11 on the clock, plenty of time to mount another game-tying drive. On its first third down, Flacco found Anquan Boldin short across the middle and Boldin turned the catch into a 19-yard gain. The next play, it was Flacco to Boldin again, this time for 17 yards and up to the Denver 36. Two short runs and an incomplete pass forced Flacco to take the Ravens' first timeout with 3:16 to play setting up 4th-and-ballgame for Baltimore. Flacco dropped back and threw a bullet to tight end Dennis Pitta. The Raven TE was blanketed by Bronco safety Mike Adams, who deftly knocked the ball away.

All Denver had to do was run out 3:12 of game clock to move onto the

AFC Championship game. Unfortunately, conservative coaching doomed Denver.

The Broncos ran with Hillman twice up the middle, gaining a first down and forcing Baltimore to call their second timeout of the half. Manning handed off to Hillman again, forcing the Ravens to utilize their last timeout. Hillman to the left for a mere one yard ran the clock to the two minute warning and set up 3rd & 7. When they came back from the break, the team handed it off for the fifth straight time to the small, untested rookie. He was stoned at the line of scrimmage for no gain.

Denver couldn't run the clock out, in part because Hillman couldn't run between the tackles and partly because Mike McCoy wouldn't call a pass play, so Baltimore had one more chance to tie.

Then it happened.

Broncos fans remember the "Fail Mary." On 3rd & 3, Flacco uncorked a deep pass down the right side of the field. Rahim Moore, who was starting at safety, ran over, stopped, jumped up—too early!—and could do nothing as the ball floated over his outstretched arm and into Jacoby Jones' hands. The lanky Jones trotted into the end zone and ended the Broncomaniacs' celebrations, pushing the game into overtime.

It was the worst play in the history of bad plays at safety to Broncos fans, one that would linger in their minds for at least an entire season. It deflated the entire stadium, took the air right out of the building and John Fox believed his players, too.

The Fail Mary *basically* forced overtime. In the coming days, many would criticize John Fox's decision to kneel on the ball with 31 seconds left on the clock and two timeouts in his back pocket. After all, he possessed the greatest comeback quarterback in the history of the league—Manning passed Elway in 2012 with the most 4th quarter and/or overtime comebacks in NFL history—and this was at home in Denver, in a playoff game.

What rubbed salt in the wound was when the Atlanta Falcons, faced with an almost identical situation—getting the ball with 30 seconds to play and two time outs—ended up scoring and winning their game the next day. (It must be noted the Falcons had to go for it, as they trailed by a point and were not tied like the Broncos.) Fox later said he knelt on the ball because he thought his team was "shell shocked" and even later said he couldn't sleep for days following the loss. He was also unapologetic for coaching conservatively.

"I think the wind out of our sails was more part of that decision than the actual wind," Fox explained of the bomb devastating his players mentally. "I'd do it again 10 times if it presented itself 10 times in that situation. Some people love comparing it to the Atlanta game. It's not close to the situation because you're going to lose the game if you don't score. Ours is completely different, because we get to fight the next round. I think that was the thinking. Obviously, it didn't get executed like we planned. But that's on the coaches and players to execute better and we didn't get it done."

So, the Broncos and Ravens went into overtime, to the next round of the boxing match, as Fox envisioned. No one could score. Each team was visibly tired, worn out, debilitated due to the grueling regular season and now this wild, wind-filled, epic playoff game.

The two teams battled on, coming to a stalemate through the first overtime period.

How often are we football fans treated to a double overtime NFL playoff game? Not very. Free football is the best kind, especially when one play, one mistake or flip of fate can decide the outcome of a season.

Onto the second overtime, the sixth quarter of football; this, after players already ran themselves ragged throughout the season. And in that second overtime, the Broncos' oldest player looked too tired to compete anymore, giving the game away.

Manning, who had been nothing short of magnificent all season long, rolled out to his right, stopped and threw back across his body, trying to fit a pass into Stokley's hands. The pass was picked off, again by Graham for his second on the day. Five plays later, the Ravens' Justin Tucker kicked home the game-winning 47-yard field goal.

Talk about a heartbreaker.

After playing so well all season long, pointing out and working hard to help correct teammates' mistakes while leading by example and making all the correct decisions week-in and week-out, Manning came apart at the seams. Throwing across your body is the biggest sin a quarterback can make. It's a mistake youngsters make, not wily veterans. It takes all the strength out of a throw because the player is off-balance. A gun-slinger needs to step into the throw, drive his shoulder through and push the football to the precise point he's aiming for. Manning made it look like a last-ditch effort, an "I give up" kind of play, on a 2nd down nonetheless. If he just takes a sack or even throws the ball harmlessly out of bounds, the Broncos line up for a third and long. If they don't get it, Denver likely punts from near mid-field and controls the field position, which was critical at this point because neither team could move the ball.

Instead, Manning threw away the Broncos' season with that interception, which was both unimaginable and incredibly ironic, given the fact he was the one most responsible for putting the team in that position in the first place. It was the start of a long, nutty off-season in which Manning and his teammates worked diligently to improve.

This game was an instant classic, one for the ages. The win helped propel the Ravens into the Super Bowl and stuck in the minds of Broncos fans and players alike for the entire year after.

What followed the 2012 Divisional playoff loss to the Ravens proved to the sports world that, no matter what comes, the Elway—Manning era is all about one thing: bringing the Lombardi Trophy back to Denver.

Consider the challenges faced by the team, the incredible ups-and-downs that may have distracted a less ably-led organization. Despite these things, the focus and dedication remained. It was palpable.

When else has there been a free agency disaster and conquest within mere days? When have two front office executives received DUIs within mere months of one another? When has a rising superstar fallen so quickly and so harshly from grace in a single offseason? What other season has nearly every single week presented as a "headline" matchup? Or where seemingly every single week, a team sets multiple franchise and even NFL records? When nearly every single game is televised nationally, with a given network's top tandem of broadcasters? Or when a head coach has to have emergency heart valve surgery and his interim head coach is rumored to be the next coach at a major college program within the same week? When a 37-year old quarterback not only plays the best season of his storied career, but better than anyone to ever lace up cleats for his unprecedented fifth NFL MVP?

It was an exciting year to be a Broncos fan, and in the end, the best year to become one.

While longtime Broncos backers may take the last few years as just another era in a long and storied history, it's simply not that. Everything about this time and place in Broncos history oozes specialness, uniqueness, extraordinariness; this is one of the greatest times in Denver Broncos history.

Why is there a need for this book? There are just far too many storylines that pop up in certain games or weeks, tales which must be highlighted. These stories deserve to be told and remembered by Broncos fans for years to come, or discovered by them in the future.

And if this book is about the Elway—Manning era, why start with the game that ended the 2012 campaign? Because I fully believe the loss to the Ravens in that legendary game set the tone for every aspect of what has come since. It left the bitter taste of defeat in Denver's mouth, and much like the home playoff loss to the Jacksonville Jaguars in January 1997, this loss heralded a relentless pursuit for vindication and greatness.

John Elway explained the similarities between the two games and his burning desire to win. "Yeah, I think that is kind of my makeup," he said in late April, 2013. "I think having been through what we went through last year—having the No. 1 seed and then lost, in 1996 when we lost. The bottom line is 13-3, we had a good year last year. It was a great year but it was a great regular season. My point is that we can't be settled with that and happy with that. The fact is we have to look at 13-3 not only as players, but as a coaching staff and even on the personnel side and try to figure out how we're going to get better. The last thing we can do is be satisfied with 13-3 and losing in the first round of the playoffs, because that is not what we want."

With that statement, Elway charged his team, challenged them to be better. It's exactly what he got in 2013 and we can only wait to see what kind of excellence he coaxes out of his team in 2014.

The 2013 season was phenomenal success, but not before a fantastic free agency period, multiple distractions and a multitude of injuries reared their ugly heads.

This is the story, the journey, of the 2013 Denver Broncos and the dawn of what has become the Elway—Manning era.

CHAPTER 2

HIRINGS AND FIRINGS:
THE FIERCE ELWAY-LED FRONT OFFICE

"To be successful, a man must exert an effective influence upon his brothers and upon his associates, and the degree in which he accomplishes this depends on the personality of the man. The incandescence of which he is capable. The flame of fire that burns inside of him. The magnetism which draws the heart of other men to him."

~ Vince Lombardi

While the Broncos players went home to rest, relax and remind themselves of the heartbreaking loss in mid-January, some were still burning the midnight oil. These men were not resting: they were laying down a strategy and deciding which dynamic moves Denver needed to make to become the best team in the National Football League.

John Elway—there is no more iconic name in Denver. The former Denver Broncos star quarterback led the team to five Super Bowls, including their first two NFL Championships. This was the man responsible for making the team one of the most loved football franchises in NFL history. The team's first ever Hall of Famer was now pulling the strings as the leader of the Broncos' front office.

To illustrate what the Duke of Denver did for football (and football fans) in the Rocky Mountain Region is far too lofty a goal for a single paragraph. Entire books have been written about just his prolific playing career and Elway is currently penning a new chapter as an executive. He was, without a doubt, the greatest player in Denver Broncos history. His 47 comebacks in the fourth quarter or overtime of contests was legendary. His "helicopter" play in Super Bowl XXXII was a microcosm of his 16-year career; with the game tied and the pocket collapsing, he flung that bruised and battered 37-year old body into three Green Bay Packers' defenders to earn a late-game first-and-goal. The play set up the go-ahead touchdown and proved that Denver's gunslinger was willing to leave it all on the field. Elway did everything in his ability to will his team to wins, be it scrambling for his life to pick up desperation first downs or firing bullets through seemingly impossible windows.

In the 80s, Elway carried the Broncos to the Super Bowl three times; at least on the offensive side of the ball, where he made the best of shorter receivers and mediocre running backs. Those teams featured feared defensive units, with Elway the lone star on offense to carry the load. Ultimately, Elway led his 1997 Broncos to their first ever Super Bowl victory, though, without Mike Shanahan's stellar coaching and Terrell Davis' dynamic running, none of it would have happened. In 1998, they did it again, earning back-to-back NFL Championships and being worshiped as gods in the Mile High City.

Elway brought his competitive fire—burning hotter than 1,000 suns—to his new position as Executive Vice President of Football Operations. He was now effectively running the day-to-day operations of the organization. Pat Bowlen was the owner of the Denver Broncos and is currently regarded as one of the top owners in the National Football League. Coming a long way since buying the Broncos in 1984, he is well respected around the league, currently holding the position of acting chair of the league's competition committee. All of that said, John Elway is the Broncos de facto owner. At the very least, he's the one responsible for the major moves going on inside the organization during this "Elway—Manning Era." Elway made drastic changes shortly after assuming the front office leadership role in Denver, which ultimately set the team up to take the

AFC's No. 1 seed and make deep playoff runs two seasons running. It's no secret Elway wanted to be at least part owner of the Broncos following his retirement in 1999, and he instead bought and founded the Colorado Crush, an Arena Football League team. Still, everyone knew Elway wanted back in the NFL and specifically with his beloved Broncos, which is why Bowlen putting Elway in power in 2011 was such a serendipitous move.

It must be noted here how nearly impossible a turnaround the organization went through following Elway's addition to the front office. In January of 2009, Josh McDaniels was hired as the head coach to succeed the franchise's most successful head man, Mike Shanahan. McDaniels inherited an 8-8 team with a franchise quarterback—whom he quickly traded away—as well as other talented players he alienated and traded or released. Brandon Marshall and Peyton Hillis come to mind. History has thus far validated some of McDaniels' 2010 draft choices such as Demaryius Thomas and Eric Decker. Even so, the greenhorn head coach was most well-known for using his second pick of the 2010 first round on Florida quarterback Tim Tebow, an athletic All-American whose mold was not of typical NFL cast.

Before we move too far forward, let's consider 2009 for a moment. Following 15 years of the best Broncos football anyone had ever witnessed, Mike Shanahan was unceremoniously fired. Shanahan had become known as "The Mastermind" for a reason; he was the offensive coordinator for the 1994 Super Bowl champion San Francisco 49ers. In that stellar Super Bowl, Steve Young passed for six touchdowns, a record performance in the NFL's championship game.

Months later, Shanahan was hired by Pat Bowlen to be the Broncos next head man. At only 43 years old, Shanny was a bit young as a head coach. The results, however, spoke for themselves. The 1995 Broncos went 8-8 in his first season, and then improved to 13-3 the next year before collapsing at home in the playoffs against the expansion Jacksonville Jaguars. There was no doubt that loss left the team hungry; it helped prepare and propel them to the next level. Denver boasted the No. 1

offense in 1997 and, after the "revenge tour" of beating the Jaguars, Kansas City Chiefs and Pittsburgh Steelers, the Broncos won Super Bowl XXXII over the Green Bay Packers. It was Denver's fifth trip to the big dance, it was their first victory. It couldn't have tasted sweeter.

1998 was "The Mastermind's" masterpiece. That team stands as the greatest in the history of the Denver Broncos for many reasons. John Elway may have been on his last legs—missing four games due to bruised ribs he sustained when Junior Seau drove his 38-year old body into the turf—but he was still one of the fiercest competitors in the league. Terrell Davis had fully blossomed at this point. Not only was he seeing the holes with ease, he hit them hard, running with confidence. T.D. scored TDs like they were going out of style; he was simply unstoppable. Those two were so great, they commanded so much focus, that others may have been forgotten. Shannon Sharpe revolutionized the tight end position, Rod Smith was the greatest undrafted receiver in the history of the league and that offensive line was annually the top unit in the NFL. After starting 12-0, the team couldn't remember how to score on a cold day in New Jersey against the Giants, losing, but simultaneously eliminated the pressure of going undefeated. That team finished 14-2, the most wins and least losses for a team in orange and blue, ever. Shanny's masterpiece team dismantled the Atlanta Falcons 35-19 in Super Bowl XXXIII; it was the perfect way for Elway to ride off into the sunset.

It is worth noting that the head coach of the Atlanta Falcons that day was none other than Dan Reeves. With as storied a football career as any single person, Reeves had become the then-youngest coach in NFL history when he joined the Broncos in 1981. In 1983, Elway was drafted by the Baltimore Colts, simultaneously being drafted by the New York Yankees. Elway would not play for the Colts and let it be known that he would choose baseball unless he was traded to one of a select list of teams—the Broncos were on that list and Reeves made sure that Elway ended up in Denver. Who would have guessed the long-term ripple effects of the trade that brought Elway to the Broncos in 1983? Here we are more than three decades later and the ramifications of that deal are still not completely played-out.

There was another prime contributor on the coaching side of the aisle during the Reeves/Elway run—none other than Mike Shanahan. In the 1980s, Shanny was Reeves' quarterback coach and then offensive coordinator. His success led to his first head coaching stint with Al Davis' Raiders; it lasted less than two years, from 1988-1989. Shanahan was let go by Davis and found himself back with the Broncos—only to be fired in 1991 as part of what was perceived by the Denver fan-base as a power struggle between Reeves and Elway. So when Elway and Shanahan beat the Falcons and Reeves that day, there was a bit more emotion to it than was perhaps apparent to the casual observer.

Following all of the history leading up to Super Bowl XXXIII, John Elway, The Duke of Denver, rode off into the sunset. He rode out on top. The man retired—through tears and snorts—and it was clear his mind was still telling him he had a little left in the tank but his body couldn't take the beating of another season. Months later, Davis' career basically came to an end, too, when Matt Lepsis rolled TD's knee trying to tackle an opposing defender.

For Shanahan, there were many years of mediocrity following the Super Bowl wins and some competitive seasons as well. Ultimately, he could never push or will the team back to the biggest stage. His revolutionary offense of the mid-90s had become stale and predictable; the game had passed Shanny by. In 2008, after going 8-8 three straight seasons and missing the playoffs all three, he was fired. It was a bit shocking because Broncos' owner Pat Bowlen had famously proclaimed Shanny had a "job for life," but even those two Super Bowls couldn't keep The Mastermind around forever.

So, in December of 2008, Shanny was handed his pink slip and the search for the next Shanahan began. Bowlen headed up the search and stumbled across someone that seemed similar to Shanahan. Josh McDaniels was the offensive coordinator for the New England Patriots at the time, a young and seemingly bright offensive mind. In 2007, his offense—with Tom Brady behind center—became the most prolific offense in the history of the league, scoring 581 points. Although he was young and wet behind the ears, Bowlen hired McDaniels at 33, making him the youngest head coach in the NFL at the time. His inexperience showed in a variety of ways.

One such way was the NFL Draft and personnel strategy in general. Simply stated, the kid was given the keys to the car, proceeded to run the car careening off a steep mountain road and laughed as the car tumbled and exploded into flames.

Within months of being hired as head coach, McDaniels had tried to trade Pro Bowl quarterback Jay Cutler to his former team, the New England Patriots. Smells fishy, right? McD and his buddy Bill Belichick couldn't get the deal done for Matt Cassel, though, and when word came out of the failed attempt, Cutler was pissed. He didn't "trust" the organization anymore and was eventually traded to Chicago for Kyle Orton, a first and fifth round pick.

In the Draft, McDaniels gambled on Knowshon Moreno in the first round; Moreno, as well as fellow first-rounder Robert Ayers, were labeled as busts four years into their careers. Then he took Alphonso Smith (who?), Darcel McBath and Richard Quinn (why?) among a host of others that aren't in the league five years later. It was a disaster. To make matters worse, he took the DB Smith ahead of Earl Thomas III, who would prove his worth as one of the best safeties in the game against the Broncos in Super Bowl XLVIII.

When the season finally started, it began with a bang. Orton connected with Stokley on a wild and unimaginable last-ditch effort as it bounced off two Cincinnati Bengals defenders' hands and Stokley was off to the races for the 12-7 win. Despite all of the head-scratching, things were looking great. The team started 6-0 before the bye, even beating the Patriots in overtime.

Then the season fell apart.

Denver lost their next four out of the bye, won two, and then finished on a four-game losing streak to miss the playoffs at 8-8. The saddest part? All they needed was one, measly win during the month of December—they couldn't beat the 5-11 Raiders or 4-12 Chiefs. It was embarrassing.

Although, not nearly as embarrassing as the next season.

Save a few standouts—Demaryius Thomas, Eric Decker and Zane Beadles—the Draft was again disheartening. And while Thomas has since turned into one of the top receivers in the NFL, his career started slowly and shakily due to Achilles issues.

Oh, and McDaniels drafted some guy named Tim Tebow in the first round. That seemed to be a big story. Tebow was a good ol' Christian boy. In between reading bible verses, he threw giant, 500-pound tires around to work out. Forget God—at Florida, Tebow was God reincarnated. He was sensational, leading the Gators to two National Championships by both throwing and running all over opponents. In the NFL, he found it a tougher time.

While there was a competition in training camp, Orton won the job and kept it all season long. Tebow did get in a few times, mostly in "Wildcat" or "Wild horses" running formation plays. That, in itself, was frustrating for Broncos fans. McDaniels spent a first-round pick on a quarterback that he only allowed to run the ball? And just a mere 12 times? Ridiculous.

When the ball was kicked off, the Broncos started 2-2. It was fool's gold. This team was nowhere near mediocre, even with a pedestrian quarterback. They were piss-poor. In fact, it was the poorest product in the history of Broncos teams. You'd have to go back to the 1960s and the AFL, when the franchise was in its infancy and struggling to survive, to find a team that rivaled McDaniels' monstrous, sickening creation. They lost seven of their next eight games and when they hit 3-9, Bowlen had seen enough. It was time to pull the plug on this failed experiment.

McDaniels was fired, but not before dumping or alienating many of the team's most talented players—Cutler, Brandon Marshall and more—and it can't be forgotten that there was a cheating scandal under his watch. While the Broncos were set to play the San Francisco 49ers in London, Steve Scarnecchia, the team's director of video operations (hired by McDaniels), taped the Niners' walkthrough. It was later found that McDaniels never watched the tapes, but he didn't turn his guy in, either.

The Broncos aren't cheaters, they never had been before. They weren't going to start. McDaniels was fired and Broncos Country rejoiced.

Running backs coach and long-time Broncos assistant Eric Studesville was given a shot as the interim man, compiling a 1-3 record while starting Tebow at quarterback for three games. Timmy Teriffic was so-so at best while throwing, and electric while running.

4-12. It was the worst the Broncos had ever been. McDaniels had seemingly driven Denver so far into the ground it would take years to rebuild the classy organization. The brand was in jeopardy and it needed rescuing—say what you want about Denver, but it is a consummate sports town and the Broncos are its first love. The team's history called for a savior. The soul of every Bronco on the Ring of Fame demanded satisfaction. The fan base itself deserved something special.

Enter The Duke of Denver, John Elway.

The Duke hired John Fox, known at the time as a player's coach. Fox was known to have a character more defined as calm, cool and collected than ferocious and furious. Kyle Orton (acquired as part of McDaniels' infamous Jay Cutler trade to Chicago) earned the starting nod from Coach Fox in training camp and promptly yawned the 2011 Broncos to a 1-4 start. Following the Week 6 bye, Tebow was installed and history began to write itself.

Tebow, known for a very strong dedication to his faith, won seven of his first eight games and took the club to an improbable 8-5 record fueled by a string of late-game miracles. Following a three-game slide to end the regular season, Denver improved to 8-8 and won the AFC West.

Tebowmania whipped Broncos fans into a manic frenzy as he led the team to a victory versus the Pittsburgh Steelers on Wild Card weekend. The game took place in Denver at Sports Authority Field at Mile High Stadium (which has come to be known as the "New Mile High"). The "Season of Tebow" climaxed with that overtime win; a victory in which even the winning play was improbable. Tim Tebow, a more naturally gifted runner than passer, threw a perfect pass to Demaryius Thomas who caught it and raced 80 yards to pay-dirt on the first play of overtime.

New Mile High was electric, the noise was deafening—I should know; I was there in the nosebleeds seats, next to a Steelers fan—and the magical ride Tebow carried all Broncos fans on seemed like it would never end. At least, we hoped it would never end, at that point and time. It was the most fun I've ever had, rejoicing with 80,000 screaming Denver die-hards. After starting the season as a backup to Kyle Orton, Tebow was thrown into the fire and performed well, going 7-4 to end the regular season and 1-0 to begin his playoff career. This unlikely success wasn't thanks to profound passing ability—his 46.5% completion percentage was 34th of 34 quarterbacks in 2011—it was attributable to Tebow's will to win, ability to use his legs and a unique knack for snatching victories from the jaws of defeat.

The Mile High Messiah certainly performed some miracles in 2011, but Elway wasn't convinced Tebow was the answer. Following the Wild Card win over Pittsburgh, Tebow and the Broncos were blown out by Tom Brady and the New England Patriots in Foxborough. The score was 45-10. No one knew it at the time, but that game marked the end of the "Tebow Era", an incredible year and one in which a mediocre team was the talk of the nation almost every day on ESPN and other sports networks. Elway knew he needed an elite quarterback to get the Broncos back to the peak of the NFL.

The single most impactful moment in John Elway's front office reign has been landing Peyton Manning in the 2012 offseason. The very next day, he traded Tim Tebow to the New York Jets. Tebowmaniacs questioned

Elway's football acumen, even though most of them were more impressed with Tebow's religious fervor than his abilities on the field.

If Elway is remembered for nothing else personnel-wise, he'll be remembered for luring Peyton Manning to the Mile High City. At the time, there were a whole host of teams going all-in for a chance at Manning. From the San Francisco 49ers to the Miami Dolphins and a few in between, he could have chosen any of them.

Landing Manning was massive, but this was only the kickoff to an explosive free-agency period. It was the marquee move in a long list of awe-inspiring acquisitions that positioned Elway's team to compete for a Super Bowl less than two years after going 4-12.

Days before the 2013 AFC Championship Game, former Broncos receiving great Rod Smith was asked if he expected the team to achieve such quick success under Elway. Here's what Elway's former teammate—who has the most catches, receiving yards and touchdown catches of any undrafted free agent in NFL history—had to say:

"Yes. One thing I'm big on is principles. I don't follow people. I follow principles," Smith said, a successful businessman himself following football, who stayed in Denver to purchase real estate, create a music studio and more. "Unfortunately, me and John were on a plane going to the funeral together for Mike Heimerdinger, and I'm watching this guy on his iPad watch every game in the NFL that week, every single game, every single play and I said, 'Oh, it's done.' He knows where to go, where to look. You know what? A lot of that came from his dad. He took that and took it to another level. That guy, he probably doesn't sleep that much because it's almost like he's on the field, but he's not. He takes that kind of care into putting this organization together, so it doesn't surprise me that the thing happened as fast as it did. Honestly, it's going to continue because he's not just building for now and going out there to try to win a championship now, he's building as well for the future. That's why some of the contracts that these guys have signed are for them for the long-haul, not just for right now."

Back to the 2012 off season. Elway signed safety Mike Adams from Cleveland and re-signed kicker Matt Prater, solidifying key positions. He then signed Joel Dreessen, Jacob Tamme, Brandon Stokley and Andre Caldwell to provide depth with versatile pass-catchers. Stokley was actually coaxed out of retirement and his rapport with Manning was well-noted. In fact, many local football analysts contend Stokley was a major reason Manning picked Denver, and I agree. The two played from 2003-2006 in Indianapolis and once both were reunited in the Mile High City, Stokley helped Manning and new receivers mesh; the veteran receiver as able to communicate expectations and help teammates understand what it means to work with Peyton the perfectionist. Elway also bolstered the Broncos' offensive line and defensive depth by signing former New England Patriots center Dan Koppen and Atlanta Falcons linebacker Keith Brooking. Every one of the players named here played a vital role in Denver's 2012 success and many were still on the team in 2013.

In the 2012 Draft, Elway found multiple starters and key backups. The class looked like this:

1) *2nd round, 36th overall: (DE) Derek Wolfe,*

2) *2nd round, 57th overall: (QB) Brock Osweiler,*

3) *3rd round, 67th overall: (RB) Ronnie Hillman,*

4) *4th round, 101st overall: (DE) Omar Bolden,*

5) *4th round, 108th overall: (C) Philip Blake,*

6) *5th round, 137th overall: (DE) Malik Jackson, and*

7) *6th round, 188th overall: (LB) Danny Trevathan.*

By 2013, Wolfe, Jackson and Trevathan were all starters, and in 2012, Hillman played a major late-season role and was a significant factor in the "Fail Mary" game versus the Ravens.

From 8-8 in 2011 with Tebow to 13-3 in 2012 with Manning and Co., there's no way Elway could out-do the 2012 free agency period—Manning is one of, if not the biggest, free agent signing in NFL history—but that didn't stop the Duke from trying to top himself in 2013.

Elway was electrifying in his continued approach of building the Broncos into a winning team. In two days—March 12 and 13, 2013 to be exact—Denver signed Wes Welker, Louis Vasquez, Terrance Knighton, Dominique Rodgers-Cromartie and Stewart Bradley. They also re-signed Kevin Vickerson.

Without a doubt, wide receiver Wes Welker was the headline name in a group of skilled and very important players. Welker built a reputation through his 10 years of professional football by being a crazily competitive, durable tough-guy despite his small stature (5'9"). He has become known as the greatest slot receiver in the history of the NFL, the numbers speak for themselves. Many people don't know this, but what makes Welker so amazing is his ability to link up with a quarterback mentally—it was Tom Brady in New England, and now, Manning—to make everything work physically and mechanically. In essence, what makes a great slot receiver is the ability to read and then run option routes (Kirwan & Seigerman 2011).

With properly executed routes, a slot man can be open on virtually every play. This is how Welker burned Broncos defensive backs so many times while with Brady, and it's how he would work to thrive in Mile High, as well. He's quicker than he is fast, more shifty and shady than long and lanky; Welker's best asset is getting in where he fits in and he quickly found a happy home in Denver. The upgrade from Stokley to Welker was mutually beneficial; Welker hit a career-high in touchdowns and the Broncos offense set multiple NFL records. Like Manning, Welker also offered intangible qualities such as a tenacious work ethic and veteran leadership. To wit, he was voted a captain by teammates and it was only his first year in the Mile High City.

It wasn't just that Elway landed Welker, it was how he did it. According to reports, as the Patriots and Welker were going back and forth through their ugly divorce, New England reached out to other teams, including Denver. Elway's front office said at the time they didn't think Welker would be a good fit. Instead, they would look to improve at the tight end position.

When the Patriots offered Welker only $10 million for two years (less than the five-year, $28.5 million dollar deal they offered to the younger and more athletic Danny Amendola), Welker opted to search for a new team. He found the perfect fit in Denver. This time, Elway jumped on Welker's availability, quickly signing the diminutive receiver to a two-year, $12 million contract. The only man to enjoy five 100-reception seasons in NFL history, when he was signed, Welker was the greatest slot man to ever suit up. In acquiring Wes Welker, Elway staged an interesting and intelligent coup against one of the craftiest teams in the league. Pun intended.

Terrance Knighton, at 6'3" and 335 pounds, promised to be the massive man in the middle of the defense, plugging up holes and commanding two offensive linemen on running plays. Part of the reason he was so attractive to Denver was the fact he played under now defensive coordinator Jack Del Rio when JDR was the head coach in Jacksonville. Due to this relationship, he was already familiar with the system and, of course, his coach. He was a big-time pick up, both in terms of his size and the way he played all season long.

Then there was Dominique Rodgers-Cromartie, affectionately referred to by fans and journalists alike as "DRC." Originally signed as a starting cornerback, this special player developed as the team's top defensive back and helped make this a special season. Champ Bailey, perennial leader in the defensive backfield ever since his trade to Denver from the Washington Redskins, was lost to an early injury. DRC stepped up to fill that void and assumed the No. 1 cornerback position gracefully. Every single week in 2013, Rodgers-Cromartie was asked to shut down opposing teams' No. 1 receivers and each week he was up to the task.

Kevin Vickerson played for the Broncos from 2010-2012 and was a key re-signing in 2013 as the starting tackle next to Knighton in the middle. At 6'5" and 328 pounds, Vickerson was able to use his size to push through offensive linemen and was a big part of the defensive line's production in 2013 through the first 12 weeks. He sustained a hip injury while facing New England and was lost in November.

Louis Vasquez, named a 2013 All-Pro, could be considered the signing of the 2013 offseason. As opined by the Broncos' own Andrew Mason (@ MaseDenver) via the Twittersphere in January 2014, "It's legit to say Louis Vasquez is the best signing in the 2013 NFL free-agent class. No other '13 FAs were 1st-team All-Pros this season. bit.ly/1qx7bgg." Vasquez became the starter when Manny Ramirez was asked to move from guard to center before the season kicked off due to injuries. If you were to ask Broncos fans, they'd most likely say Welker was the biggest signing of the 2013 offseason, however, becoming an All-Pro in your first season with a new team is something extraordinary indeed.

In one day, Elway landed five players capable of starting on a Super Bowl-caliber team. This is the stuff legends are made of. And, Elway pulled it off two years in a row. Still, it doesn't seem too good to be true because, well, it happened. And this is John Elway we're talking about here, the fabled football player who was largely responsible for putting the Denver Broncos on the map. Despite his on-field accomplishments and legendary status, possessing the professionalism and charisma to go out and convince five game-changers to join the cause is simply sensational.

Of course, Elway and Manning are about the most dynamic football sales team anyone could ever run into. Hell, Elway wasn't like a used car salesman, he was one; at least, in another lifetime. The Duke of Denver has since sold his multiple car dealerships, turning his attention to his beloved Broncos, a team he is re-establishing as a perennial powerhouse. And there's no questioning Manning as one of the top three QBs in the league. Plus, Peyton is well regarded as one of the finest pitch-men in all of sports. From fronting brands such as Papa John's, Buick and Sony he helped define the new brand and sell fellow players on the latest incarnation of the Denver Broncos. In 2012, while Denver found its way onto multiple nationally televised games, Manning spoke highly of the organization, his relationship with Elway and their commitment to winning. His representation of the team and its progressive new style of competing must have helped the squad add all the talent they did in such a short time.

Following Welker, DRC and Knighton's signings, Denver went from feeling a mile high to an even more elevated state. It was announced they had re-signed their biggest free agent, Elvis Dumervil.

We were to learn that just wasn't the case, however. In a wild twist of fate, Dumervil's agent—Marty Magid—sent back his player's signed contract too late, preventing the defensive stalwart from rejoining the Broncos. "Fax Gate" was upon us.

In a world filled with smart phones that can text, email and tweet, the $9 billion business that is the NFL allows its players' futures to be decided by fax machines. Do people, in 2013, even know how to operate a fax machine? Apparently the answer is yes, but everything didn't work out the way Denver wanted.

What Elway and the Broncos wanted was for Dumervil to take a pay cut from a $12 million salary in 2012 to $8 million, gaining the team $4 million in salary cap space. Elway was an able negotiator, persuading veterans to sign "hometown" deals where they would accept a salary lower than that commanded by the market in exchange for a higher probability of winning a championship. Based on the logic that Denver was one of the most talented teams in the league and an NFL Super Bowl was more likely here than elsewhere, Elway was able to retain talent that may otherwise have been lured away.

It was basically a snowball effect; Elway stood atop the Rocky Mountains—the day-to-day decision maker of one of the most fortuitous football franchises—and started the ball rolling when he signed Manning. That move grew exponentially into other deals when people got a glimpse of what he was capable of doing on the field post-surgery. Everyone wanted to play with Peyton as he went for a career-ending Super Bowl, just as Elway did 15 years prior. Who wouldn't want to walk away from the game as a champion?

Elway was one of the blessed few to do so; many others wanted that same storybook ending.

Not Dumervil. The defensive end didn't want to take a pay cut and ended up accepting an offer from the Ravens. The irony for Broncos' fans was that "Fax Gate" precipitated Dumervil's signing with the very team that beat the Broncos in that classic, double overtime "Fail Mary" game. It wasn't just that they lost Dumervil—a man they drafted in 2006, who had been phenomenal for them ever since—they also lost one-half of the most feared pass-rushing duo of 2012.

On top of that, Denver had to still pay Dumervil $4.8 million dollars; Elway wasn't happy about it.

"All I can say is there was a 1:00 deadline," Elway explained of "Fax Gate." "I don't like the fact of how everything ended up, but obviously Elvis made the choice of what he wanted to do in free agency. He chose to go where he wanted to go. Before that, I would say that if there's anything I would take back it's the fact that if there's a deadline, there's a deadline. There's a reason why there's a deadline, because you can't get everything done fast enough. It's an unfortunate situation, but that won't happen again."

With Dumervil lost to Denver's newest rival, Elway was pissed. He didn't waste time searching for Dumervil's replacement. Welcome veteran free agent Shaun Phillips. Phillips had terrorized quarterbacks in orange and blue for nine seasons with the San Diego Chargers, but some feared that, at 32-years old, he was past his prime. It wasn't the case; Phillips turned into a consistent pass-rushing threat for the 2013 Broncos. In fact, he out-performed Dumervil (10-9.5 sacks) and only cost Denver $1 million. Yet another testament to Elway's wheeling and dealing as a front office guru.

Denver lost Dumervil to Baltimore by trying to cut his salary. Another irony of the situation—this is exactly why New England—another modern-day rival—lost Welker to the Broncos.

Then there was the 2013 NFL Draft. As expected, Elway and his front office comrades looked to further build and bolster the future of the team.

To summarize, the class looked like this:

1) *1st round, 28th overall: (DT) Sylvester Williams,*

2) *2nd round, 58th overall: (RB) Montee Ball,*

3) *3rd round, 90th overall: (CB) Kayvon Webster,*

4) *5th round, 146th overall: (DE) Quanterus Smith,*

5) *5th round, 161st overall: (WR) Tavarres King,*

6) *6th round, 173rd overall: (OT) Vinston Painter, and*

7) *7th round, 234th overall: (QB) Zac Dysert.*

In the first round Denver had the 28th pick and chose defensive tackle Sylvester Williams, an All-American from North Carolina. It was the right move because the Broncos needed defensive line depth, but was he the right guy? Williams couldn't find the field much for most of his rookie season, finally getting consistent playing time after starters were injured. Second rounder Montee Ball was heralded as one of the big names at running back in the draft. The big back played well in his rookie season, complimenting starter Knowshon Moreno well. Webster was taken in the third round and also found playing time due to injuries. The Broncos draft was rounded out with a quartet of players who have yet to make a significant impact anywhere in the NFL: defensive end Quanterus Smith, receiver Tavarres King (now with Carolina), tackle Vinston Painter and quarterback Zac Dysert.

Other key preseason re-signings included punter Britton Colquitt to a three-year deal, special-teams captain David Bruton, center Dan Koppen, safety Duke Ihenacho, tackle Chris Clark. Backup running back C.J. Anderson was also signed as an undrafted free agent.

Elway wasn't done there. As injuries pop up, executives are expected to fill the voids. The front office excelled at scouring the waiver wire, searching for capable veteran replacements and promoting effectively within their own ranks.

Putting their noses to the grindstone wasn't all the Broncos' brass was doing, though. There was plenty of partying going on, too. Would poor judgment among the executives taint the Broncos' season before it even began?

CHAPTER 3

Broncos Brass Gone Wild

> *"Morally, the life of the organization must be of exemplary nature. This is one phase where the organization must not have criticism."*
> *~ Vince Lombardi*

It was the summer of 2013 and everything seemed to be going swimmingly in Denver.

After going 13-3 the year before, John Elway and his front office cohorts used the early offseason to build the Broncos into one of the most talented teams in the league through both free agency and the draft.

Where they were weak in 2012, Elway bolstered deficiencies. The defensive line depth was increased with Knighton, Vickerson and Williams, while the same could be said about the secondary with DRC, Jammer and Webster. Vasquez, Clark and Koppen all proved to be valuable offensive linemen and Welker was the cherry on top.

And when I say Elway did all of this, it's just because it's easier—or maybe more fun—to envision Elway kicking his feet up on the big desk in the huge office inside Dove Valley. I like to imagine the Duke, smoking a cigar and sipping scotch, calling the shots and calling other team's GMs in search of deals.

Growing up in Denver as a kid when Elway was still throwing the football around Mile High Stadium, he was a god; we even sang about him. In our D-town rendition of the song about a reindeer with a red nose, we finished, "You'll go down in history...like John Elway!" No joke.

It must be noted—and must be somewhat obvious—he had help. There's no doubt he is the face of the franchise on the administration and business end of things. Even so, there are key front office contributors we don't normally hear much about.

Those men are Tom Heckert and Matt Russell, among a total of 19 people listed on the Denver Broncos official website as part of the player personnel/football operations side of things. Here's how the hierarchy breaks down: Pat Bowlen—Joe Ellis—John Elway—Matt Russell—Tom Heckert.

Unfortunately for them, the first time many fans heard of either Heckert or Russell was in June when the news of their separate drunk driving incidents broke out.

Spirits were certainly a mile high that summer; apparently the front office was, too.

First, the news came out regarding Matt Russell's DUI on July 8. The very next day brought word of another DUI within Denver's front office, this one going to Tom Heckert. Each story was sad and stupid in its own way.

Heckert was the first of the two to receive a ticket for driving under the influence of alcohol. This incident occurred on June 11 in Parker, Colorado.

Russell's was much more severe. His DUI, which took place on July 6 in Summit County, had more details released; they weren't pretty and were in fact a bit scary. While on his alcohol-fueled joy ride, Russell reportedly hit two cars, including rear-ending a Breckenridge police car. When he was tested, Russell's blood alcohol content was reported to be 0.246; the legal limit in Colorado is merely 0.08. Testing out at 0.246 is frat-boy wasted, it's "I'm 21 and don't know my limits" wasted. As Colin Daniels quipped via Twitter, ".246 is drinking schnapps all day wasted." According to the arrest affidavit, police recovered a half-empty bottle of peppermint schnapps in Russell's car at the time he was pulled over following the two accidents.

These are grown men in their 40s. Operations professionals tasked with the responsibility of running an organization that is part of a league with a drinking problem. It's ludicrous that they conducted themselves in such poor fashion given everything they were supposed to represent.

Every year there are reports of NFL players getting DUIs—running back Knowshon Moreno was arrested for DUI in February of 2012, former Broncos linebacker D.J. Williams made the same mistake while with the team in 2010 and so on—and they keep on happening. These executives are supposed to set an example for the twenty-something athletes they employ, young adults who oftentimes find themselves with a surplus of money for the first time. Honestly, if you were 21 or 22 and filthy rich, you'd probably blow a significant portion of your signing bonus partying, too, right?

This isn't to say young adults shouldn't party—they will, many of us did—but they must have the responsibility and common sense to call a cab after drinking. We all know they can afford a cab ride. The same goes for the more senior members of the organization, especially when they're the ones in charge, nearly atop the hierarchical ladder.

What's more, the NFL has gone to great lengths to keep their players from drinking and driving, even putting in place their own driving service for players and other personnel alike.

The Broncos released a statement following Heckert's arrest which in part read, "Tom's actions are obviously part of a disturbing pattern of irresponsible behavior that we are aggressively addressing within our organization. One member of the Broncos arrested for driving under the influence is one too many. This type of behavior puts innocent people at risk and cannot be tolerated. While our team and league supply plenty of resources to prevent these situations, it is clear we need to do better. We are thoroughly reviewing the procedures we have in place and will do whatever it takes to enhance their effectiveness going forward."

And then another after Russell's arrest. This time, "Our organization is extremely disappointed and concerned with the incident involving Matt Russell. We immediately expressed our disappointment to Matt, and he is fully aware of the seriousness of this situation. This type of behavior is unacceptable and very troubling. We expect better from all employees, particularly those in leadership positions. These allegations completely contradict the values and beliefs of the Broncos regarding social responsibility. We are continuing to gather information and will handle this matter appropriately and in accordance with all NFL policies."

The team went into full-on image-healing mode; they had to deal with the PR nightmare Russell and Heckert created in the middle of the dog days of summer.

"These are egregious errors," Broncos' President Joe Ellis said following the DUIs. "The only good thing is nobody was seriously or critically hurt. Both employees have been on the record expressing their remorse, and that's all well and good. But it's not going to prevent us from addressing this in the right manner. Executives in our company are held to a higher standard. That's a mandate handed down from the commissioner. One episode is one too many. Two is ridiculous. I understand the outrage in the community; I understand the outrage of the fans. It's justified. We have an obligation to do the right thing. And we will."

And since this type of error in judgment is usually made by players, it created an interesting dynamic where players wanted to see how the executives would be treated and reprimanded.

"It's particularly disappointing that two members of my staff acted so irresponsibly," Elway said in a statement. "Simply put, it's unacceptable and inexcusable."

"The front office is just as accountable as the players are going to be," Elway said in reference to players looking on to see what the punishments would be for executives.

Heckert was suspended 30 days without pay. Russell was suspended indefinitely on July 15. Two months later, near the beginning of the regular season on September 14, Russell was reinstated. In some ways, the punishments were too light; others are fired for doing something as sophomoric as this.

They spent the rest of the season with the team and the public relations nightmare seemed to vanish into the Mile High thin air. Neither executive faced further consequence. What seemed like huge stories, especially when presented together, died out quickly when another, larger drama developed in Denver.

CHAPTER 4

Von Miller is a star

///

> "You never win a game unless you beat the guy in front of you. The score on the board doesn't mean a thing. That's for the fans. You've got to win the war with the man in front of you. You've got to get your man."
>
> ~ Vince Lombardi

Miller's not just a star in the sense of being an all-world football player—which he is—but Miller's a star in the dramatic sense as well.

After sacking opposing quarterbacks, Miller loves to perform his many celebratory dances, taking advantage of the spotlight if only for a few, diminishing seconds. In 2012, after a pick-six versus Tampa Bay, he didn't disappoint with a spirited dance in the end zone; his six forced fumbles that year gave him even more opportunity to make his presence known.

He's a good looking youngster, with a big, bright smile and those signature square-framed glasses that give him a feeling of smarts. He's a national salesman, or at least, was for a time. Why?

Because when it came to the offseason of 2013, the unfolding Von Miller Melodrama was fodder for a national football audience.

Magnificent was Miller's play on the football field. In his first two seasons, he pillaged other teams' offensive lines, ransacking quarterbacks on a whim. He was the greatest thing to hit the Denver defense since John Lynch. As he was drafted by Denver, the Broncos got him at his absolute best.* During the first 9 games of 2012, Miller logged 30 quarterback hurries (along with 10 sacks).

While Lynch was an all-time great, making the finalist list for the Professional Football Hall of Fame at the end of this season, he came to Denver as a player in the twilight of his career.

But they wouldn't have been in the position to draft this trench warfare specialist if it weren't for being very bad, first.

After their terrible 4-12 season in 2010, Miller was the No. 2 overall selection by John Elway's front office. It was the highest draft pick in the history of the franchise and it was Elway's first NFL Draft as an executive. Talk about pressure.

But Elway's legend was forged in the fire; due to undergoing a tremendous amount of pressure and seemingly always coming through in the clutch, he shines like a diamond. So did Miller.

Elway could have taken Patrick Peterson, a supremely talented cornerback and punt return specialist, or defensive tackle Marcell Dareus. In the end, Elway stuck with his gut and went with Miller. It was the right choice. Through three seasons, Dareus has totaled a mere 18.5 sacks, Miller had that many in 2012 alone. While Peterson has been a very good contributor—including four touchdown-garnering punt returns in his rookie year—he was not on the level of greatness Miller was reaching.

In his rookie season, Miller was a sensation, exploding onto the scene by harassing quarterbacks and creating turnovers. Week 1 versus the Raiders heralded potential greatness as Von forced a fumble on the first snap of his pro career. 2011 saw Miller rack up 11.5 sacks, tying a Broncos rookie record. He added two forced fumbles, four passes defended and 50 total tackles. So dominant was his performance that Miller was named not only Defensive Rookie of the Year, but also earned his stripes as an All-Pro in his first NFL season.

It was only a sign of things to come.

Without a doubt, Miller improved and became the Denver defense's MVP during the 2012 season. Miller was a pass-rushing machine that year, usually utilizing his patented speed-rush, but also able to stunt or power-rush a guy straight on. Much like other stars in the National Football League, Miller is a physical freak of nature; he stands at 6'3" and 250 pounds, with the speed to run a 4.5 40-yard dash and a 43" vertical leap as recorded at the NFL Combine. In fact, he was the top linebacker performer six out of seven drills at the 2011 Combine, another indicator of his potential ability to dominate the opposition.

With that big and speedy frame in a two-point-stance, Miller possessed the explosive first step that allowed him to be on an offensive tackle before the would-be blocker was ready to deal with him. Many times, No. 58 took the long way, going wide outside of the tackle, getting low and blowing past even the best blockers in the game.

In the Broncos' second game against the San Diego Chargers that season, Miller enjoyed his best game of the year. He made his primary antagonist, Jeromey Clary, look lost on the football field. On one sack, Miller simply ran around Clary; the offensive player was so incredibly outmatched versus this burgeoning superstar he seemed to be stuck in quicksand. On another play, Miller juked once, juked again and made the Chargers' longest tenured lineman—Clary—look like he'd forgotten how to play as he took Philip Rivers down once more. Three sacks on the day tied a career-high; he even stripped Rivers twice for fumbles that Denver recovered.

With Miller on one side and Elvis Dumervil on the other, the Broncos led the NFL in total sacks (52, tied with St. Louis). All of that pressure created opportunities for turnovers through the air and on the ground.

In fact, Miller was so masterful attacking offensive tackles and quarterbacks that he was in the running for Defensive Player of the Year. He stood out despite playing opposite of Dumervil and was eventually beaten out by J.J. Watt of the Houston Texans. Interestingly, while Watt had more tackles (69 vs. 68), sacks (20.5 vs. 18.5) and passes defended (14 vs. 2), Miller forced more fumbles (6 vs. 4) and also had his pick-six versus Tampa. Watt did not record a pick-six. At the time, I thought Miller deserved the award because he proved to be an all-around disruptive defender, filling up the stat line even more than Watt did. Voters didn't agree, though, giving Watt 49 votes to Miller's one.

Still, those 18.5 sacks set a new Broncos record and he was named an All-Pro for the second time in two years. Specialty? Professional terrorizer. He was the greatest edge-rusher in the storied history of the franchise. In 2012, there were no signs of slowing down, only the possibility of improvement.

Until everything came crashing down.

Fast forward to the summer of 2013 and Miller's popularity plunged.

Much like a shooting star, Miller came out of nowhere to light up the night sky; conversely, he seemingly plummeted to Earth in a fiery conflagration just a short time after capturing the attention of so many.

And then, on July 22, 2013, exactly a week after the team suspended Russell and Heckert for their DUIs—it was reported that Miller would be suspended for four games.

"Seeing reports abt 4 game susp. I know I did nothing wrong. I'm sure this'll be resolved fairly. Disapp. Broncos have 2 open camp like this," Von Miller tweeted that day.

According to that same NFL Drug Policy, a four-game suspension only comes after moving to "Stage Two" and then failing another test. If that were the case, his tweet may have been a bit of a stretch.

This was no simple problem, it seemed; as the reports came out, we saw just how much trouble the youngster had gotten into. It was possible that his suspension could get worse, much worse.

On August 11, Miller was arrested while trying to purchase a firearm at a Centennial, Colorado gun store. He had a warrant out for his arrest due to a driving infraction in October of 2012. The offense was careless driving, driving without a valid license or insurance; the details were first reported on by local ABC outlet, 7NEWS Denver (TheDenverChannel. com, 2013). According to those court records, Miller was supposed to appear in court on December 31, the day after their final regular season win over the Kansas City Chiefs. The warrant was then filed on January 2. He was brought in after the warrant was discovered during a background check while attempting to buy the gun. Although immediately released on $1,000 bond, the episode was another black eye on the youngster's reputation.

A few days later, Miller met with the NFL Players Association and the league in Washington DC to try and work out a lesser suspension. After hours and hours of deliberation between the two sides, the league decided Miller would be suspended for six games of the 2013 season. As it turned out, he originally tested positive for two different drugs during his rookie season, but it never came out in the media.

Miller was caught poppin' Molly—as the kids say—and smoking marijuana. Molly, an amphetamine and party drug, along with marijuana, were banned substances. It was a shocker the rising star would be so foolish.

Then, in the 2013 offseason, he spilled a urine sample. This was quickly followed by his attempt to work with an employee of the testing facility to dilute another sample. Each infraction was a violation of the NFL's Substance Abuse Policy.

The ban began on August 31 and lasted until October 14. It could have been as much as an entire year, if it weren't for that negotiating by the NLFPA along with the unique nature of the infractions.

"Obviously we're frustrated with what's happened—and I think disappointed in Von," Elway said of Miller's suspension. "I think the way that I've looked at this, and we'll continue to look at this, is the fact that the decision that's come down—we'll live with that decision. What I'd like to do is try to do everything we can to prevent any other situations. Whatever we have to do as an organization to try to help Von, we want to be able to do. Put aside the fact that he's a good football player—him as a person. And it's time that if we can get him help, to help him take that next step in the maturation process, we want to do that. We'll take it one step at a time and the first step now is to make sure that we're getting Von the help that he needs to get."

"Everybody is going to have to step up," Head Coach John Fox said of losing his edge-rushing master for the first six games. "I know it is, 'Next man up,' but he's a hard man to replace, [and] the guys around him have to play better. The guys on the other side of the ball have to play better and that'll be the challenge to our team."

This says a lot about the perceived impact of losing Miller, arguably the team's second or third-most important player behind Peyton Manning. Not only was Fox afraid it would affect the defensive line's ability to pressure the quarterback, but it even reached over to the offensive side of the ball. They'd have to score more and keep the opposing offense off the field because No. 58 was out.

That day, Miller was asked about how the legal trouble and suspension had affected his relationship with the fans. "My true fans, true Broncos fans, they've been great. Coming out to practice, still believing in the guy that I am," Miller explained. "The media, they can do some crazy stuff to you and paint a different picture. But the fans that know me for going out there, laying it all on the field, being a great teammate, entertaining the fans and just being the fun Von—that's who I am, that's who I've always been, that's who I'll continue to be."

It wouldn't end there for Miller though; the guy simply could not stay out of trouble.

In September, Miller was again sited for a driving offense. This time, as first reported by CBS Denver, it was driving with a suspended license (denver.cbslocal.com, 2013). And then in October, he was nearly two hours late to the court hearing (CBSsports.com, 2013).

As 2013 and a chance at redemption approached, a mere two weeks before the season was set to kickoff against the Super Bowl champion Baltimore Ravens, Miller found himself suspended for the first six games.

Denver's Super Bowl aspirations took a major hit as they did in training camp.

CHAPTER 5

TRAINING CAMP
UPS-AND-DOWNS AND PRESEASON PROSPECTS

> *"Perfection is not attainable. But if we chase perfection, we can catch excellence."*
>
> ~ *Vince Lombardi*

Ah, training camp.

The dog-days of summer are filled with two-a-day practices in the sweltering sun, studying playbooks and intense training in the weight room.

Training camp may seem boring to the casual observer, but it's necessary for a team to successfully prepare for the upcoming season. There were many players that needed it in 2013. Take Duke Ihenacho, for instance. The previously undrafted safety learned the ropes and gained confidence on the practice field, then elevated his play in preseason action, basically forcing coaches to give him the starting nod. Julius Thomas was another young man that took full advantage of training camp, not only learning the plays but gaining an understanding of the demands Peyton Manning can put on pass-catchers.

Camp opened on July 25 and ran through August 15 that summer.

Manning was already in mid-season form when it came to talking to the media.

"I'm all in on 2013," Manning said after the first training camp practice of the year. "Guys have put the time in. Had a good season in the weight room with Luke [Richesson], our strength coach, and now is the time to put that work into fruition a little bit."

"We've got a new receiver, Welker, I don't know if you saw him out there today," Manning joked. "You'd love to have five years to get that timing down. We've got a short amount of time, and that is why every day is really so important."

For a player that prides himself on precision passing and perfect timing, Peyton understands that hard work in the preseason is what leads to success in the regular and post-seasons. While he had a year to build chemistry with Demaryius Thomas and Eric Decker, that's simply not enough time to perform at the highest of levels.

Others needed to improve and fine-tune, as well, and training camp would offer plenty of opportunity to make progress.

Running back Montee Ball—along with his fellow rookies—had to figure out what it meant to practice at the professional level.

My brother, our friend John and I attended training camp in late July. A record-sized crowd stretched with the team; this tradition is not surprising in Colorado, America's fittest state. During the practice, it was clear to see how fast and athletic Demaryius Thomas was, how professional Manning was and how Ihenacho's intensity impressed everyone.

But, as they ran 11-on-11 drills, a major injury occurred. On a play designed to position him as the lead-blocker on a run, center Dan Koppen tore the ACL in his left leg. Given that the center is perhaps the most important player on the offensive side of the ball outside of the quarterback, it was a potentially devastating blow to the team. The center touches the ball on every play, ensuring it finds its way safely to the QB. Continuity and familiarity between the center and QB is necessary.

The Broncos were fortunate to even have Koppen. After spending his career in New England helping that team to three Super Bowl championships, he was cut in August, 2012. The Pro Bowler subsequently signed with the Broncos in September after then-center and Broncos product J.D. Walton injured his ankle. The injury required surgery and kept Walton on the Physically Unable to Perform (PUP) list. During Peyton's time in Denver, he hadn't had much of an opportunity to form this all-important bond.

So, almost on the fly, Manny Ramirez moved over from right guard to center. Ramirez had been signed in January 2011, having spent the bulk of his professional career to that point as a back-up in Detroit. Immediately, there were mistakes. Two fumbled snaps on a practice drive alone were cause for concern. Ramirez went from career backup to starter at right guard for Denver in 2012—with many missteps along the way—now he'd be taking on an even more important role as the team's center. Besides hiking the ball and having to be on the same page with Peyton, who loves to change plays as well as snap-counts, Ramirez was responsible for making protection calls to teammates in the trenches before Manning called "set."

The only reason Ramirez was asked to start in 2012 was because Chris Kuper—arguably the team's best offensive lineman—also severely injured an ankle. By the time training camp started in 2013, Kuper still wasn't back to full health. When Ramirez moved from right guard to center, the ripples reached out to touch the entire offensive line. Louis Vasquez, coming off the bench, would now be starting at his regular right guard spot. Interestingly, Ramirez and Vasquez played alongside one another in college, at Texas A&M, which was beneficial because it meant less time was needed for the two players to gel. The duo became the strength of Denver's offensive line as the season went on.

Of course, there were bumps and missed snaps along the way. The Broncos went so far as to lure Ryan Lilja out of retirement to see if he could play center. Lilja, a former teammate of Manning's in Indianapolis, was traditionally a guard. He ended up as the fourth-stringer behind

Ramirez, C.J. Davis and Steve Vallos. Lilja never saw the playing field as a Bronco. But it was a sign the team wasn't certain Ramirez could be the full-time starter.

About a week later, with Ramirez and the rest of the new offensive line—as well as the entire team—getting more practice time together, the Broncos gathered inside Sports Authority Field at Mile High Stadium for their annual summer scrimmage. They were greeted by the best fans in football.

An unseasonable downpour of rain fell on Denver that August afternoon, delaying the scrimmage for 40 minutes due to lightning and thunder. The weather couldn't dampen the spirits of the most dedicated fan base in the league, though, as 44,439 Broncomaniacs danced, cheered and watched as their favorite athletes played in the rain like children.

Nearly the entire team took turns sprinting, diving and sliding head-first on New Mile High's turf. "I felt like a kid," Manning said after the scrimmage. "I don't know when the last time I got a chance to do that was, in a professional venue like that." And fans had probably never seen something like that, either.

It was a heartwarming moment. All the stress and pressure of pushing to win a world championship slipped away for those few minutes in the rain. Fans were treated to the spectacle of grown men playing as if they were in grade-school; professionals who were joyful just to be out there playing the game they loved.

Some work actually got done, too, with the first-team defense playing against the second-team offense and vice versa. It was the first time the team had engaged in real contact including hitting and tackling in full pads. The crowd was impressed, especially when Manning connected with Demaryius Thomas in the end zone for a touchdown on a particularly impressive play that saw DT fully extended to make the grab.

When the first depth chart came out a few days later, there were a few surprises. First, with Knowshon Moreno still working his way back from an ACL tear he sustained late in 2012, Ronnie Hillman and Montee Ball were Nos. 1 and 2 respectively at running back. Hillman got some good work in during his rookie season, but was he really the best back on the team? At tight end, it was Joel Dreessen and Jacob Tamme, no mention of Julius Thomas. And at safety, the starters were Mike Adams and Rahim Moore ahead of Duke Ihenacho and David Bruton.

How things had changed.

In the week leading up to the preseason opener, Stanford announced they would retire John Elway's Cardinal No. 7 on November 7. A well-deserved honor and only one of three numbers ever retired in Stanford's storied history (the other two belonging to Ernie Nevers and Jim Plunkett).

On August 8, the Broncos flew to San Francisco for their preseason opener. As is customary for many starters in the first preseason game of each season, Manning played only one drive. C.J. Anderson, who was far behind his teammates on the depth chart at running back, enjoyed 69 yards on 15 carries. Julius Thomas also impressed, catching a team-high four passes for 35 yards. But the Broncos opened their scoring on defense, as Nate Irving knocked the ball loose and Shaun Phillips' nine-yard fumble return touchdown gave the team a 7-3 lead in the 2nd quarter. Matt Prater added a 46-yard field goal in the fourth and Denver forced four turnovers on the day to win 10-6.

Another standout in the game was Duke Ihenacho, who led Denver's defense with seven tackles and a forced fumble. He flew to the ball, just like safeties are supposed to do, and it seemed inevitable that he would soon be a starter. He was playing himself into a starting spot as the preseason went on.

Ryan Clady, who tore his rotator cuff in Week 17 of the 2012 season, was getting back into playing shape by participating in practice once again. His situation basically mirrored Chris Kuper's, who severely shattered that ankle the year before. Unfortunately, while those two big men were feeling better, budding runner C.J. Anderson's season came to a close when he injured a knee blocking in the final training camp practice of the year.

And during those training camp practices, Denver Broncos die-hards were in full force. Not only did a record 44,000 fans attend the open practice at New Mile High Stadium, but a total of 86,364 were present and accounted for throughout camp. That's simply remarkable; 86,000 people went to watch practice.

Practice? We're talking about practice, man.

We're talking about practice.

After camp was done, on August 15, Manning commented on the work that was put in.

"I think the best part is knowing that we got a lot of good work accomplished," Manning said. "It has been a physical camp. We are in full pads just about every day, which certainly can take a toll physically on players, but guys have pushed and worked through that. It's the only way to really get a real idea of what kind of team you are going to have and how guys hold up in full contact."

Well, if preseason games are any indication of regular season success, the next contest wasn't a positive sign. And, little did anyone know at the time, but it was a glimpse of the future.

The Broncos went to Seattle to play the Seahawks, which was shaping up as one of the better teams in the league. Seattle put on a profound performance that night, completely dominating Denver all-around.

Preseason Predictor

The Broncos started with the ball and went three-and-out to begin the game with a big Kam Chancellor hit on Wes Welker on third down to force the punt. Seattle answered with a long drive capped off with a touchdown. On the drive, Russell Wilson connected on many short passes, including the 12-yard TD throw to Jermaine Kearse. Wilson fumbled the ball before the throw, but in a show of athleticism, he picked it up and still scored. Fans saw the lightning-fast young QB adjust the ball, get a grasp and throw a dart.

7-0, Seahawks.

With Moreno still resting due to his knee rehab, Hillman and Ball were given the majority of the carries. It was disaster for Denver.

When they got the ball back, the Broncos earned a first down. But on their fourth play, a 20-yard pass from Manning to Julius Thomas turned into a fumble and Chancellor returned the ball to Seattle's 46. The next play was a 33-yard gain on a go route down the right sideline for Golden Tate to the Denver 21. The Broncos defense stopped Seattle's attack and forced a 42-yard field goal by Steve Hauschka, the kicker who had been waived by the Broncos in 2011.

10-0, Seattle.

Denver's offense finally found a rhythm; Hillman's running was ineffective, but Manning's passing to Welker and Julius Thomas went for 12 and 18-yard first downs respectively. On 3rd and 5, Manning threw it short to "Orange Julius," who took the ball and rumbled 31 yards to the Seattle 15. Two plays later, Manning found Welker in the end zone for the first time in a game.

10-7, Seahawks.

We were given a glimpse of how great this offense could be. Although, no one thought they could play that well throughout entire games, and certainly not week after week all year long. Of course, that is exactly what happened. The Juggernaut was gathering strength.

Just as the Broncos captured the momentum, though, Kearse made another impact, taking the kickoff 107 yards to the end zone.

17-7, Seattle.

Denver took the punch and fought back, marching methodically down the field. There was a heavy dose of Hillman on the drive and he seemed to be gaining confidence with every gain of positive yards.

Then, it happened.

With the Broncos threatening to score from the one-yard-line, Hillman was handed the ball. The small back was hit hard, fumbling into the end zone. Seattle's strength–their physicality–showed early and often in the preseason contest. Brandon Browner picked the fumble up and instead of kneeling it—which is what most players would do—looked to run it out and went 106 yards for another Seattle touchdown.

24-7, Seattle. Early second quarter.

Denver answered with another three-and-out, while mixing in an illegal formation and offensive pass interference penalties. After a 33-yard punt return by Tate, the Seahawks were in field goal range. Hauschka made the 41-yarder.

27-7, Seattle.

Wilson gunned in another touchdown just before halftime; who was this guy?

34-7, Seattle. Utter domination.

When Manning and most of the starters went out after playing a half, his numbers were quite good. 11-16 for 163 yards and one score, but even his play may have not been enough to bring the Broncos back that day.

In the second half, Seattle's backups continued to beat down the Broncos' bench guys; the overall performance was indicative of that physical supremacy that the Seahawks would come to be known for during the upcoming season. Seattle ultimately won 40-10.

What came from this game? We were able to see a few things result from the contest; consequences that only add to the greatness of the year. Indeed, the interconnectedness of the season and many of its teams is wild, whacky and wonderful all at the same time.

First and foremost, Jermaine Kearse played so well, he was able to cement a spot on the Seahawks' roster and then help beat the Broncos later in the season. His 107-yard kickoff return for a touchdown was his first *attempt* at a return since high school. He told reporters after the game that he considered telling his coaches "no" when asked if he could still return. Kearse also had the 12-yard touchdown reception from Wilson, proving his versatility and value to the team.

Maybe more importantly from a Broncos perspective, John Elway jumped on his team following the loss. The Duke was not pleased, and he let his team know about it in the locker room, behind closed doors. This was his team and he demanded excellence; that it was a preseason game was no excuse. While reports of Elway stepping into the locker room to yell at the team didn't come out until late January, it illustrates an important piece of the puzzle regarding Denver's historic season.

Elway lit a fire under players and coaches alike, ripping into them and reiterating the goal of winning the Super Bowl.

"What I said was if you want to win a world championship, you don't go anywhere and lose 40-10," Elway explained in late January, 2014. "To me, it seemed like some people thought it was okay, so I made sure to say it wasn't okay. At least I didn't think it was okay."

"John pretty much laid it on us after that game, that was a butt kicking," Manning said to the media in late January. "He talked about what he thought our potential could be and didn't want to see that wasted. I think guys got the message.

"He might have been giving a message to coaches as well as the players and everybody in the room got the message," Manning continued. "It was the first time he had addressed the team and when he had something to say it was important."

Something else of note: Broncos defensive end, Derek Wolfe, was lost during the game to a scary injury. Only minutes into the game, Wolfe was cut-blocked. As he tried to get up and make a tackle, the fullback ran through the hole and hit him with furious force in the head and neck. Wolfe lay on the field motionless for nearly 10 minutes as "Greek" (head trainer Steve Antonopolus) and the rest of the Broncos' training staff looked over the large man. He was eventually placed onto a stretcher and into an ambulance on the field to be rushed to the hospital. Wolfe was quickly tweeting that he would be okay and back to the field soon. How sadly wrong he was.

Usually the third preseason game each season is most telling for a football team because their starters traditionally play the most amount of time of any preseason game. While they were only active for the first half of the loss in Seattle, hindsight tells us it was clearly the most important preseason game and as such, the most deserving of analysis.

Days after the smack-down in Seattle, news of Von Miller's suspension broke. To say it was a distraction would be an understatement. Teammates reacted after the news came out.

Wesley Woodyard was a team captain and the expectation was for him to start at the weak side linebacker spot across from Miller. Woodyard broke it down from a team point-of-view. "We've got to take care of our business and Von has to take care of his business, on and off the field," going on to say, "we've got to continue to be good teammates and support him. Whether it's four games, no games or six games—we're going to still be there for him."

"We hate to say that it's 'next man up' for those two guys [Miller and Champ Bailey, who was injured against Seattle] because they are our best players on our team," safety Rahim Moore said. "But at the end of the day, other guys are going to have to step up."

It created a bit of a conundrum for the Broncos at linebacker. Miller was to start on the strong-side and Woodyard at weak-side; then the team signed Paris Lenon to play in the middle when Miller's suspension was announced. Really, you don't replace a talent like Miller; he's a massive man with incredible athletic abilities, a once-in-a-generation type talent.

"Any time you lose a player like Von, it's going to hurt you, but to be a great football team—this isn't going to be the last bump we have this year," Elway said in reaction to the suspension. "There are different things we're going to have to go through, that we're going to have to deal with."

Oh, how prophetic Elway's words would end up being.

At the end of the day, Woodyard moved over to middle linebacker, Nate Irving was working on the strong-side and Danny Trevathan on the weak-side—at least during camp. This meant an expanded role for Shaun Phillips at edge-rusher. Yes, Phillips, the 10-year veteran free agent Elway signed before the season to a cap-friendly $1 million, one-year deal would prove to be incredibly important. At first, it seemed as though Phillips would take over for Dumervil, instead, he'd be filling in for Miller.

Confidently, Phillips talked about needing to step up, "Pressure can either break you or pressure can make diamonds. We're going to continue with the philosophy that pressure is going to make diamonds for us. We'll be quite alright."

Indeed, the defense was alright—not great—and they were able to play well without Miller in the lineup for most of the season.

"What you do is you take adversity and you turn it to a positive," Phillips continued. "That's our mindset and that's what we're going to do."

That's exactly what this team did all year long, and it's likely the Miller melodrama had that impact. Losing their star defensive player to suspension was the second wake-up call of the preseason, strengthening the Broncos' resolve. Later in the year, players would talk about fighting through all the adversity this particular season presented; while there were already multiple major injuries to Dan Koppen and Derek Wolfe, the first major signpost, if you will, was Miller's suspension.

That Friday, the entire team and most of the coaching staff met with fans during the second annual Kickoff Luncheon. They discussed football over lunch with the Denver die-hards that couldn't wait for football to begin, with multiple silent auctions' proceeds going to benefit Mile High City charities.

On Saturday, the third preseason game kicked off. It was the first home contest for the Broncos. The St. Louis Rams came to town and presented a tough test for the usually most-important exhibition contest. The Rams scored first, set up by a phenomenal punt return from Tavon

Austin who took the ball to the three yard-line. Manning, however, led the offense down the field to answer (although not without some drama). With the ball on the Ram six yard-line, Denver decided to go for it on 4th and 2. Manning rolled out right and threw a perfect strike to Demaryius Thomas in the back corner of the end zone.

With Denver down 10-7, the Broncos started in the shadow of their own end zone. Manning dropped back and threw to Hillman in the flat; he was hit, held up and stripped of the ball by Alec Ogletree. Ogletree then picked up the pigskin and rumbled in for the touchdown. St. Louis led 17-7 thanks to another fumble by Hillman. The Broncos put a field goal on the board and then tried to come up with points before halftime with a last-minute drive. An errant Manning pass fell short of Julius Thomas and was picked off by…you guessed it, Alec Ogletree. The Rams turned it into another field goal, leading 20-10 at halftime.

Interestingly, Miller started the game and played the entire first half with the starters, even though Coach Fox and everyone else knew he'd be suspended for the first six games of the regular season. Why not tweak the defense and prepare to play without Von? It was a move Fox was criticized for in the media after the game.

Out of the locker room, the starters showed life with backup Brock Osweiler at quarterback. He hit Demaryius Thomas a few times and Knowshon Moreno split time with Montee Ball, who pounded in a touchdown, finishing off a 79-yard drive. The Broncos were now down 20-17. With the rain pouring down, Lerentee McCray blocked a St. Louis punt and the Broncos took over at the 15, leading to three points and the tie at 20s.

Denver took the 27-20 lead in the fourth quarter on a run in which Lance Ball wouldn't be denied, and won the game by a margin of 27-26 in dramatic fashion. St. Louis scored a TD late and had the chance to easily tie the game and force overtime; Head Coach Jeff Fisher instead elected to go for two points and the win and was denied by a wall of orange and blue.

"We were still able to win, that's the bright side," Fox said after the game. "The not-so-bright side is that we got four turnovers and that's something we worked on very hard last week, and we'll work on very hard again this week.

"When you have young players learning to play in this league for the first time it can happen and we have to eliminate that before the first game of the regular season."

Turnovers. Against Seattle, four turnovers helped the Seahawks bury the Broncos. Four more turnovers allowed the young Rams to hang in and almost beat the Broncos at home. And in their first preseason game, forcing four turnovers by the 49ers helped Denver win the close contest.

Turnovers. More than any other statistic, turnovers are the most important variable in any winning formula; a team on the positive side of turnover differential—takeaways minus giveaways—will likely win. Add in explosive plays, and the most statistically accurate indicator of wins can be utilized. More on this newly developed statistic—one you're going to want to know about—at the end of the book.

After the game, the team made cuts down to 77 players, with most of the 11 drops being either rookies or second-year players. Two days later, safety Quentin Carter was placed on Injured Reserve (IR) and center J.D. Walton was added to the PUP list. The roster was trimmed to 75.

In late August, the NFL and their 4,500 retired players who were suing the league due to complex issues surrounding the historical handling of concussions settled for $765 million dollars. At the time, critics said the players could have and should have held out for more money; after all, they argued, the league was making more than $9 billion per year. The settlement also cleared the NFL from ever having to divulge information about those particular cases, which was damning evidence. The league moved to protect itself and did so with the massive settlement, just weeks before the 2013 season kicked off.

The fourth game was what you would expect from the last exhibition of the preseason; Manning and many of the starters didn't play, while most of the backups and special team spots were ultimately decided by individual performances. Even a strong touchdown run couldn't earn Jeremiah Johnson a roster spot, though, as he gave the Broncos an early 7-0 lead. A 27-yard field goal by Matt Prater and it was 10-0, Broncos. Ryan Williams from the Arizona Cardinals answered with a tough touchdown run of his own—on a fourth down. In the second half, third-string Broncos QB Zach Dysert connected with receiving hopeful Gerrell Robinson for a touchdown. The beautiful play-action completion led to a 17-10 lead. This would be short-lived. Arizona's backups out-played Denver's and the Cardinals ultimately won 32-24.

Only one day after their final preseason game, the Broncos had to make many more roster cuts to get down to the game-day limit of 53. Both Johnson and Robinson (5 receptions for 99 yards and the score) seemed to be on the bubble, each of them could have made the team due to those strong performances in the preseason finale.

Neither made the squad.

Lance Ball, Ryan Lilja, Johnson and Robinson were the most notable names of 18 to either be waived or released, three more were placed on Injured Reserve and Miller was suspended.

One of the standouts in preseason that not only earned a roster spot, but also a starting spot, was Duke Ihenacho. Amazingly, he actually went from undrafted free agent to scout team player in 2012 to starter in 2013.

"It definitely lights a fire under me," Ihenacho said of going undrafted in 2012. "Every day I go out to practice I have to prove myself because everybody knows that undrafted players have to fight an uphill battle compared to other players. That's not an excuse or anything—I just take it as a challenge and I'll keep rocking."

He's the type of player a football team loves to have, one that works diligently to improve all the time. Ihenacho's not stagnant, he's not worried about labels being placed on him and he's simply working his tail off to be the best football player he can be. If that means passing up "should-be" starters, so be it.

"We're going to try to pick the 53 best guys that we think can help win us a championship," Head Coach John Fox said after their final preseason contest. Without wavering, Fox, Elway and the entire Broncos' leadership constantly spoke of winning a championship as their ultimate goal. While it seems almost like "coach-speak" or lip-service, it became clear—especially as the year wore on—that Denver was in fact on a 'Super Bowl or Bust' run.

"I think that you need the veterans but the bottom line is that we kept the best 53," Elway said of keeping more young guys than older players. "Everyone says you want to win now and I say *we want to win from now on.* There's always that thought process and where we are on the offensive line with the guys we have, the guys being banged up a little bit they're getting ready to come back. We just thought that those were the best 53 we could keep."

Again, Elway reiterates the drive to be victorious, but here he changes the Broncos' mindset from "Super Bowl or Bust"—which has been a Denver motto since at least the 80s—to "Chasing Lombardi." Over and over again.

The statement "We want to win from now on" built up conceptual momentum as the season went on, and maybe it will turn into a rallying cry for Elway the front-office-man extraordinaire. Or maybe "Chasing Lombardi" will be the motto. Only time will tell.

And, as Fox was asked about the pulse of his team going into the regular season, he answered in an exuberant way.

"It's all good. I like this team," Fox said. "I like the way they've gone about their business, the way they've worked. You've got to be sick or dead to not be excited for opening day, no matter what city you're in. Of course they're excited. And to be able to kick off the NFL season makes it even more exciting against the defending world champs."

That's right, not only were the Broncos kicking off their personal season, but they were to kick off the entire NFL regular season (versus the Baltimore Ravens) as the very first game of the year.

Before they could kick it all off, Denver designated their team captains—a rather dubious distinction this particular season. Four of the five men—Ryan Clady, Wesley Woodyard, Champ Bailey and Peyton Manning—were injured, and David Bruton's special teams unit was anything but special all year long.

Still, all that lead-up was over. It was finally the first week of the regular season, a time Broncos fans, coaches and players alike couldn't wait for. It was time to strap on pads and helmets and strive for excellence. While the year might not have been aligned for ultimate redemption, Broncos fans were about to be treated to the writing of history during this sensational, historical and special season.

CHAPTER 6

NFL Kickoff

> *"In order to succeed, this group will need a singleness of purpose, they will need a dedication, and they will have to convince all of their prospects of the willingness to sacrifice."*
>
> ~ *Vince Lombardi*

This year presented a special opportunity.

Not only would the Broncos be kicking off their season at home on national television, but they'd be kicking off the season for the entire league.

What made it even better was Denver getting their chance at revenge against the Super Bowl champion Baltimore Ravens. This was the same Baltimore team that eliminated the Broncos from the 2012 playoffs due to a shocking late-game meltdown by Manning & Co. and some heroics from an impassioned Ravens team backing Ray Lewis in his final season. It was almost poetic that Denver would have the opportunity to exercise those demons on opening night.

The game also presented an opportunity to play against a former teammate, a man that spurned their team in favor of another. In early 2013, following the devastating defeat at the hands of the Ravens, Elvis left the building. Dumervil, a career-long Broncos player to that point, went to Baltimore during the aforementioned "Fax Gate" nightmare. The Broncos showed on opening night why he should have stayed.

The lead-up to kickoff was something else. The NFL went through downtown Denver—specifically the famous downtown commercial district on the 16th Street Mall—hanging banners of both Peyton Manning and Ravens quarterback Joe Flacco.

Some, like CBS4's Vic Lombardi, actually took to the streets and defaced the Flacco banners, though there was a much larger one still hanging at the stadium.

Yes, the league decided to hang banners the height of Sports Authority Field at Mile High Stadium, both of Manning and Flacco. Fans were outraged. Images of Flacco's "Fail Mary" throw to Jacoby Jones danced in Denver die-hards' heads. They didn't want him celebrated on the outside of their stadium—the same field of battle where, of course, he rose to the occasion to defeat the favored Broncos only eight months before.

Really, Broncos fans should have felt lucky; the Super Bowl champions are supposed to kick off the season at home, not on the road. But the Baltimore Orioles of the MLB had a game that weekend, so the Ravens had to fly to the Mile High and play on the road to start the season. This is the reason that the banners were hung—the league was doing what they could to create a pseudo-neutral atmosphere since the Ravens were, by right, the deserved home team. It didn't prove to be enough to make the visitors feel at home.

The Ravens probably wished everything about that night was different.

To start out, there was a freakish lightning storm that delayed the game 33 minutes; after the natural pyrotechnics, Manning lit-up the Ravens. The venerable field-general conducted a magnificent orchestra, the likes of which had not been seen during the modern era of professional football. Tying a long-held record, the man of the hour threw for an NFL record seven touchdowns.

While the Broncos undoubtedly wanted revenge, make no mistake, these weren't the same two teams that met up back in January. Dumervil, Denver's second-best pass-rusher, had switched sides. So did Brandon Stokley, who was vital both in bringing Manning to the Mile High City and in helping the quarterback acclimate to his new team.

The Ravens were without Ray Lewis, who retired following their Super Bowl run. Lewis was true to his word, hanging up his cleats just like he said he'd do before their win over the Indianapolis Colts in the Wild Card round. Ed Reed was gone too, meaning two of their most feared and most vocal leaders had left the defense. In fact, seven defensive starters from that Super Bowl XLVII winning team were gone. It showed.

Denver was also less than whole. The team was playing without Von Miller which required massive adjustments. That night, Manning wouldn't let his team lose again to the squad who ended the Broncos season seven months before. He put on the performance of a lifetime.

Manning's Magical Seven Touchdowns

After the lengthy delay—which was quirky by itself—the rain continued to come down. Manning wore a glove, much like he did during most of the rest of the season when the weather went bad.

Despite their ability to put up a massive amount of points, the Broncos started slowly due to being out of their element—due to the elements. Manning noted after the game that the weather delay threw off the team because it disrupted their usual pregame routine. It was easy to see; Denver didn't score a single point in the opening quarter and were down 0-7 at the end of the first. Joe Flacco, who was one of the most hated football players in Denver at that moment, started off the scoring with a two-yard pass to tight end Vonta Leach.

Meanwhile, the Broncos' first three drives ended like this: punt, punt, punt. What happened next was something special—the defense inspired the offense to get going and then spurred them to even greater heights as the game progressed.

After Denver's third punt, Flacco tried to hit Stokley. Instead, Chris Harris Jr. jumped in to pick off the pass. Starting at Baltimore's 24,

Manning took only one play to capitalize on the turnover; he pumped to Eric Decker on a fake bubblescreen and found Julius Thomas running wide open up the seam for the team's first score. It was 7-7, midway through the second.

Interestingly, while looking back at the game film, I noticed it was similar to other plays they ran later in the year. Both Thomas and Welker—who was lined-up outside of the tight end—ran an out-and-up. When the linebacker bit on the out route, it left both Thomas and Welker running parallel go routes, with only one safety to cover them both.

Baltimore looked to answer. But, the defense held and forced the Ravens to boot the ball away. When Welker was sent deep to receive, though, he muffed the punt. Baltimore recovered at the one. Ray Rice punched the ball in on the next play. The score was 14-7 Baltimore with 8:03 until halftime.

Manning heated up. On the next drive he had three long passes. 13 yards to Demaryius Thomas. 44 yards to Orange Julius, then 23 yards to the tight end again. The score was tied at 14.

After the two teams exchanged punts, Denver's defense bent but didn't break and Baltimore put a field goal on the board just before half. The Ravens led 17-14 at the intermission.

It was the last time they'd be ahead all night.

Manning was a man possessed in the second half, but not before Dumervil had his say. Elvis sacked the old gunslinger for a loss of seven yards on the team's first play from scrimmage. Five plays later, Manning perfectly led Andre Caldwell into the end zone on a fly for the 21-17 lead, one they would never relinquish.

Smelling blood in the water, the Denver defense was like a school of sharks; Nate Irving hit Rice hard behind the line for a loss on a crucial play and Shaun Phillips sacked Flacco, forcing a punt. The Ravens couldn't get the ball away as special teams captain David Bruton blocked the boot, setting up a five-yard TD from Manning to Wes Welker. 28-17, Denver.

Baltimore got the ball back, but their confidence had vanished in the thin, Mile High air. Their starter, Ray Rice, was also gone due to injury. Backup Bernard Pierce was ineffective and an incompletion by Flacco meant a second straight three-and-out.

The Broncos jumped into the no-huddle and Ronnie Hillman ran wild to keep Baltimore off-balance. That drive was capped by yet another passing touchdown. Manning rolled out and again found Welker—he was left wide open at the goal-line as a crossing route by DT sprung him. 35-17, Broncos. It was one of the first times the Broncos ran the crossing route; they'd use it over and over again throughout the season, finding much easy success until the ultimate contest.

Both teams were cold to end the third quarter, and it looked like Denver would walk to a win.

When the Broncos got the ball back early in the fourth, Manning put a nail in the Ravens' coffin.

Demaryius Thomas ran a stutter-go, physically fighting through the cornerback to get around him, when No. 18 dropped in the pass with precision. DT stretched his arms out, ran through the end zone and "Mile High jumped" into the first row of fans as the stadium erupted in elation. This may not have been the *exact* Ravens team that beat the Broncomaniacs' squad last year, but blowing them out still felt just as joyful.

Flacco and the Ravens were now in desperation mode, down 42-17 with time ticking away. The reigning Super Bowl champion quarterback was intercepted once more; this time by linebacker Danny Trevathan. Trevathan took off down the sideline—he'd surely score—but no, he celebrated too early and dropped the ball behind himself before crossing the goal line. In recent memory, it is the only play more bone-headed than Rahim Moore's attempt to stop the "Fail Mary." Luckily for Trevathan, the play was mostly inconsequential to the outcome, though it did spur a shift in momentum in the Ravens' favor. Baltimore scored their final touchdown on the drive following the touchback.

They put a field goal on the board a few minutes later, but it was too little, too late.

While every other play was a near-perfect pass by Peyton, on the seventh TD, it was much more Demaryius Thomas than Manning. Well, of course, Manning had to set it all up, yelling—over and over again—"Ally!, Ally!" at the line of scrimmage. He saw something in the way the Ravens lined up that told him the bubble screen was there for the taking.

Starting in the shotgun, Manning called the cadence, "Hurry, hurry. Set!", and snapped a throw to Thomas. Welker made the crucial block on the corner, Ryan Clady hustled to get another block and DT turned on the jets to go 78 yards to the house. But wait! There was a flag on the play. Manning, already most of the way down field, couldn't believe it. The foul, though, was offsides, on none other than Elvis Dumervil.

The Broncos blew out the Ravens, 49-27, and quickly became the favorites to win Super Bowl XLVIII.

Seven has always been a magical number in football—it's the number of points you earn by scoring a touchdown and an extra point, and it's John Elway's old number—to see Manning throw for seven touchdowns seemed impossible. It was a feat only believed because I saw it with my own eyes, one that was awe-inspiring. And what made it even more special was the fact that every single touchdown was different. Peyton proved to the league he and the Broncos were no one-trick ponies; four different receivers caught TDs and every scoring play was unique.

Manning and his men made it look way, way, too easy, exacting some sense of revenge on the Ravens—on national television—while simultaneously showing themselves off as Super Bowl favorites.

The win was special, and it was the perfect way to start the season. There was a feeling this was going to be Denver's year, even that early, if Manning could put up video game-like numbers against that defense.

When Manning threw for seven touchdowns, it was the first time in 44 years, since Joe Kapp of Minnesota showed up big against the Baltimore Colts (weird coincidence) on September 28, 1969.

Who were the others to throw for seven TDs in one game? The remainder of that short list is comprised of: Sid Luckman, Adrian Burk,

George Blanda, Y.A. Tittle and later in the season, Nick Foles. Besides Kapp,Burk and the youthful Foles, the rest of the list is legendary.

While he became the seventh NFL quarterback to throw for seven TDs in one game, he was only the second to do so and not throw an interception. The other man to accomplish the feat was Y.A. Tittle.

The Ravens loss by 22 points was the most ever by a defending Super Bowl champion in their season-opener.

For Julius Thomas, it was his first ever touchdown. And then second ever. Despite it being his third year in the NFL, Thomas was hampered early in his career by an ankle injury, barely seeing the field at all and catching a mere one pass in his first two seasons. In this season-opener alone, he hauled in 5 receptions for 110 yards and two TDs. This was a promising start.

It was also Wes Welker's introduction to the end zone as a Broncos player. As the year went on, would he prove as effective in orange and blue as he had been in New England?

CHAPTER 7

Peyton's Homecoming

> "Once you agree upon the price you and your family must pay for success, it enables you to ignore the minor hurts, the opponent's pressure, and the temporary failures."
>
> ~ Vince Lombardi

Peyton Manning's magnificent performance against the Ravens was only a sign of things to come for both he and his team.

Denver's offense was dynamic, dominant and despotic throughout the first six games of the season. They hung 49 on Baltimore, which was only the beginning. Peyton and his friends bullied little brother Eli Manning in his house, Broncos 41 - New York Giants 23. Unfortunately, the team lost All-Pro left tackle Ryan Clady to a lisfranc (mid-foot) injury during the win; it was a major injury to arguably the team's second-best player.

Week 3 was a 37-21 rout of the Oakland Raiders, the first divisional victory. It was also the team's first win against a former coach, as Dennis Allen—the defensive coordinator in Denver in 2011—was now the Rai-duhs' head man.

Then, the Philadelphia Eagles came to the Mile High City in a matchup that pitted the best offense in football versus the offensive "genius" Chip Kelly. Kelly, a Rookie NFL head coach, had brought his quick-tempo attack from the University of Oregon to the NFL in 2013. Kelly's Eagles could score—his offense was predicated on running more plays than the other team, way more—but it was Manning who set the tempo. The Broncos posted 52 points—affectionately known as a "50 burger" in the NFL—a rarity even in these offensive-dominated times.

Through the first quarter of the season, Denver was a perfect 4-0. They out-scored opponents to the tune of 179-91. This was the most exciting offense we'd ever seen. It was the most exciting offense anyone had ever seen.

In early October, the team flew to Dallas to face Tony Romo and the Cowboys in "Jerry World" for the first time ever. Jerry Jones, billionaire owner of "America's Team," built Dallas Stadium in 2010 at the cost of $1 billion. It was the most expensive stadium in the history of sports at the time, boasting a 60-yard-long Jumbotron, field-level suites and platforms for dancers to perform on during the contest. But fans wouldn't be caught up in all that extravagance on this day; the most fascinating entertainment was the football game itself.

Dallas brought their A-game, jumping out to a quick 14-0 lead in the first quarter. But the Broncos struck back with four touchdowns in just over a quarter's worth of time, 16:38 to be exact. Three passes went from Manning to three different receivers, then the wily veteran ran a naked bootleg—faking the handoff and taking the ball the long way around— untouched and into the corner of the end zone. It was his first rushing TD in a Broncos uniform and his first since 2008. It was as if he was telling teams, "Now you have to plan for that, too." At halftime, it was 28-20 Denver.

A quick score out of the half meant the Broncos were up 15.

But the 'Boys wouldn't roll over and die, far from it. Terrance Williams burned Tony Carter for an 82-yard score, and then Tony Romo connected with Dez Bryant and Jason Witten in succession to take the 41-38 lead.

Romo threw yet another touchdown, and his Cowboys seemed to control the pinball game, up 48-41 in the final quarter.

True to form, the Broncos mounted a massive drive capped by a Knowshon Moreno touchdown run to tie it up. With the game on the line, Romo differentiated himself from Manning—and the rest of the league's few elite QBs—by attempting to force a pass between three defenders. Wesley Woodyard picked it off, setting up the Broncos' game-winning field goal. It was a sensational shootout, a 51-48 win for Denver to remain undefeated. Those 48 points were the most ever scored by a home team in a loss, and Romo's first 500-yard game ended in disappointment, too.

The next week should have been an easy win over one of the worst teams in the league—the Jacksonville Jaguars. But the Jags performed their best against the Broncos, even bruising and battering Manning, who sustained an ankle injury. Despite the valiant effort, Jacksonville ultimately lost 35-19.

It wasn't just that the Broncos were putting up massive numbers, Manning and his crew were flying a mile high, scoring in a vast number of ways.

To start the season, the Broncos were seemingly unstoppable. Never mind the somewhat shaky defense that showed up against the Cowboys and forget that sad special teams unit which allowed big returns almost every week; this was an offensive juggernaut, the likes of which had not been seen in the National Football League.

It was jaw-dropping to watch Manning go to work and make it look elementary every Sunday.

It was simply sensational, awe-inspiring even. Manning didn't throw an interception until the fifth game, capturing a new NFL record 20 touchdowns thrown before the first INT.

Everything built towards Peyton's homecoming in Indianapolis.

It wasn't something Manning was taking for granted—excelling at the highest level—or even simply being physically able to play football. When he was severely injured in 2010, resulting in those four neck-fusion surgeries and sitting out the 2011 season, the reality was that one of the greatest quarterbacks in NFL history may have unceremoniously thrown his final pass. Manning went through with those surgeries; then the man known for being the hardest-working player in the NFL worked even harder. He had to somehow, someway regain his strength, to once again play at the highest of levels.

In the week leading up to the Colts game, Peyton was asked to evaluate his time with Denver, explaining:

"Well, I've worked hard in this new chapter of my football career. I've put a lot of time in and it's been extremely difficult."

"I've put a lot of time in," he reiterated.

"As I've said over and over again, I've had a lot of people help me in this second chapter and I'll never ever cease to be grateful for that help. So I put a lot of time into it. I've learned that in life, you need to be at peace with other people's decisions that affect you, that you have no control over. I think that's been good advice that I've had over the years, and it's certainly served me well in this particular scenario. But like I said, I've put a lot of time in.

"I've enjoyed, as I've said, getting back on the playing field. Last year (2012) was a gratifying feeling to get back and play. You miss not being in the huddle. And this year there has been enough change with the new offensive coordinator (Adam Gase) and a new slot receiver (Wes Welker) and a different tight end (Julius Thomas) to keep you kind of energized and on your toes with all the different changes. So I'm certainly enjoying playing football again. And when you're out of a job, you've got to go find another job, and Denver offered me one and I took it and they sure have helped me in my new job."

Still, knowing everything Manning had gone through just to be back on the field and understanding how important the quarterback was to his team's past successes, Colts' owner Jim Irsay fired shots that many interpreted as inflammatory.

"We've changed our model a little bit, because we wanted more than one of these," Irsay said in an interview with *USA Today* mere days before kickoff, showing off his Super Bowl XLVI ring. Manning was the Super Bowl MVP that day and the longtime leader of the Colts, making it peculiar that Irsay would say such a thing.

"(Tom) Brady never had consistent numbers, but he has three of these. Pittsburgh had two, the Giants had two, Baltimore had two and we had one. That leaves you frustrated," Indianapolis' Irsay continued.

"You make the playoffs 11 times, and you're out in the first round seven out of 11 times. You love to have the *Star Wars* numbers from Peyton and Marvin (Harrison) and Reggie (Wayne). Mostly, you love this."

See, all of the most competitive owners in the NFL are "Chasing Lombardi," in pursuit of that elusive trophy and the extravagant Super Bowl ring that comes along with its glory.

Irsay has always been an outspoken owner. While many are much more reserved, Irsay will let everyone know what he's thinking. Without a doubt, one of the most difficult decisions he's had to make as an owner was cutting Peyton Manning, the same player he took No. 1 in the NFL Draft way back in 1998.

Rewind back to 1998 and the Colts were crummy. They'd been that way for years and years. In the 10 years before Manning, the team went to the playoffs only twice, including a 1-15 1991 season. Their 3-13 record in 1997 set Indy up with the No. 1 pick, and in Manning's rookie season, they again won only three games.

But, starting in 1999, the team went to the playoffs in 11 of 12 seasons with Manning behind center. He revolutionized the way NFL offenses were run during that decade of dominance. Audibling at the line of scrimmage had been part of football for many years, but Manning took changing the play on the fly to the next level. He was a master of reading and reacting to defenses, slicing and dicing them to bits.

That's exactly how his Colts demolished Mike Shanahan's Broncos teams in 2003 and 2004, 41-10 and then 49-24 in back-to-back postseasons. Manning threw for four and then five touchdowns, respectively, all while disrespecting Denver's D. They were two of the worst playoff losses in Broncos history, certainly two of the most memorable beat-downs during the Shanahan Era, postseason or otherwise.

A few years later, in 2006, Manning led the Colts to their first Super Bowl appearance since 1970, when the team was still based in Baltimore, Maryland. The Colts beat the Bears 29-17 on a rainy February day in Miami, Florida. Irsay's team was on top.

In fact, fandom for the team grew greatly during the Manning Era in Indianapolis. No. 18 jerseys filled the old stadium in Indy and fans got quiet when their offense was on the field so that their general's marching orders could be clearly heard by his troops.

The Colts' success during Manning's first decade with the team resulted in Irsay being able to erect a sensational, state-of-the-art stadium. Interestingly, Lucas Oil Stadium's official nickname is "The House that Peyton Built." And inside "Peyton's House," Irsay and Indianapolis were able to host Super Bowl XLVI.

Still, Irsay bad-mouthed his former franchise quarterback, the very man who was so responsible for the team's resurgence. That's like flying a man to the moon and then complaining it went too slowly. It was borderline insane by Irsay.

The next day, Broncos head coach John Fox fired back at the Colts' owner, telling Pat Kirwan on his XM radio show, "I saw the comments. And to be honest with you, I thought it was a bit of a cheap shot," Fox said. "To me, in my opinion, they were disappointing and inappropriate."

"Peyton would never say anything. He's too classy to do that," Fox continued. "They sounded a little ungrateful and unappreciative to me. For a guy who has set a standard, won a Super Bowl, won four MVP awards… be thankful of that one Super Bowl ring, because a lot of people don't have one."

Including John Fox, who was celebrating his 25th anniversary of coaching in the NFL, at one level or another. In fact, Fox led his Carolina Panthers to the Super Bowl in 2003—in only his second year as a head coach—and was beaten in heartbreaking fashion, in the final seconds, by the New England Patriots. Two and a half decades is a long time to do something and not be considered the best; Fox's firing back hinted at his displeasure in not winning a ring and also at Irsay's not knowing how good he had it.

It amounted to a hyping-up of one of the biggest games on the entire 2013 NFL schedule.

Just the fact that Manning was returning home to face his former team—the only team and only NFL home he'd ever known—was enough to make this a juicy matchup. The game was positioned on NBC's Sunday Night Football for the entire country to see. But Irsay's trash talk of disappointment and Fox's feedback only helped to create an awesome atmosphere.

Of course, it helped that these were two of the best teams in the league, adding to the intrigue.

Denver put their perfect 6-0 record on the line against the 4-2 Colts, who were hungry after losing to the San Diego Chargers on Monday Night Football the week before. They were two of the best teams in the AFC, led by two of the better quarterbacks—the old gun-slinger against the youngster that took his job. What's juicier than that?

As the two teams took the field, Indianapolis—antithetical of their owner's remarks—put on a classy tribute to Manning. He was there, midfield, waving to the adoring fans as they gave him a loud and rousing, standing ovation. It was a heartfelt welcome for one of the greatest players in the history of Colts football; Manning was visibly emotional, tapping his chest pads as if to tell the 62,000 in attendance, "You touched my heart."

That's where the good feelings for the friend-turned-enemy ended, though.

The Indy crowd wasn't cheering when Manning hit Eric Decker twice in a row for Denver's first score and the 7-0 lead, that's for sure. Like every week before, it seemed far too easy for the Broncos' offense, putting a touchdown on the board in two plays; would they run the score up on the

Colts, too?

Not exactly.

With Denver leading 7-3 and controlling all momentum, Trindon Holliday caught a Pat McAfee punt, ran backwards and then toward the sideline where the football was ripped from his grasp. The ball spun wildly and stayed in bounds where Sergio Brown picked it up and ran into the end zone. After review, the Colts were awarded the ball at the 11 yard-line—Brown had stepped out of bounds—but Luck tossed it to Darius Heyward-Bey on the next play, allowing him to run circles around Champ Bailey for the score.

Holliday had an instant chance to make up for his fumble and took the ball out of the end zone from eight yards deep on the ensuing kickoff. It looked as if he'd break free and score a touchdown, too, until McAfee ran him down and blasted him on the sideline. Luckily for Holliday, the offense capitalized and scored on a Manning to Julius Thomas TD. The score gave the Broncos a 14-10 lead early in the second quarter.

In that quarter, though, Manning was strip-sacked by former teammate Robert Mathis. Chris Clark, who was starting at left tackle for injured All-Pro Ryan Clady, watched Mathis use him and then abuse Manning; after the furious hit to the quarterback's throwing arm, the ball fluttered into the end zone and was ruled a safety to the Colts. 14-12, Denver.

After the free kick, Luck did everything in his power to lead a touchdown drive—including a magical scramble on 3rd and 11 for a clutch first down—Stan Havili caught a Luck pass, running outside and into the end zone. It was 19-14, Indy.

Then, as if he was proving to the world, "This is my team, now," Luck masterfully led a half-ending touchdown drive in just 1:25. Clearly, he'd learned a thing or two from Manning—long considered one of the best at running the two-minute drill—throwing short pass after short pass to take what the Denver defense was giving him. All Manning could do was watch and pray the D would hold up. On 3rd and 1 from the eight, though,

Luck found tight end Cory Fleener for the score and a 26-14 lead at the break.

Out of the half, Luck did what Manning was never known for, he surveyed the field only to tuck the ball and run it in. 33-14, Colts.

It'd be quite the comeback if the Broncos were going to win, and they gave it their best.

A discontented Denver team committed multiple penalties to start their next drive—Mathis was held by Clark on the way to another sack of Manning—but the Maestro orchestrated a long, methodical scoring drive, anyway. Unfortunately, when Eric Decker caught the ball and reached it to hit the pylon, the official incorrectly called it incomplete. Matt Prater was called on to kick home the 31-yarder; 33-17, Indy. The Broncos were visibly frustrated for the first time all year. They were mad at the bad call, but also upset at their inability to play at the highest of levels, as they had become accustomed.

In the fourth, the Colts answered with a 52-yard kick by Adam Vinatieri to lead 36-17.

Manning had enough. Conservative short passes weren't enough. On his next opportunity, he stepped up and uncorked one deep down the middle to Decker, who tipped the ball to himself for a 49-yard gain. Two plays later, Demaryius Thomas adjusted to a poor pass by Peyton, reeling it in for the score. After a failed two-point conversion, Indy led 36-23.

Finally, the Denver defense came through; Duke Ihenacho stripped running back Trent Richardson and recovered the pigskin deep in Colts' territory. Still, the offense was off. It took them four plays to pick up a first down—a contested short pass to Wes Welker—before Knowshon Moreno ran the ball up the gut for the TD. It was now 36-30 in Indy's favor with 8:44 to play.

On the ensuing drive, Denver sent an all-out blitz against Luck on third down; the venerable Reggie Wayne was wide open but Luck threw it short and incomplete. Not only did the Colts have to punt, but to add injury to insult, Wayne tore his ACL and was lost for the year.

So, with seven minutes to play, Peyton had plenty of time to lead a game-winning drive.

It just wasn't meant to be.

On first down, Eric Walden power-rushed Orlando Franklin to hit Manning's arm as he threw, the ball floated into Colts' linebacker Eric Angerer's arms for the interception. Still, the defense held Indianapolis to a field goal, 39-30, Colts lead.

Manning pushed the ball up field with precise passing to Wes Welker but Ronnie Hillman was stripped at the three yard line. With just over three minutes to go the fumble basically ended the Broncos' hopes of winning.

Denver added a field goal, but ultimately lost 39-33.

It wasn't just the Broncos' first loss of the season, it ended their 17-game regular season winning streak, which dated back to the 2012 thrilling comeback over the Chargers in San Diego.

Interestingly, Luck out-played Manning; it was the first time anyone outshone Peyton all season. In Indianapolis, the praiseworthy performance meant a ceremonial passing of the torch, from one generation's franchise player to the next.

Why did Luck outperform Manning? And, ultimately, why did the Colts beat the Broncos?

Multiple deficiencies arose during this pivotal game, just as they did throughout the entire season.

First and foremost, Manning wasn't given ample time to read the defense, nor to make throws. The offensive line was dominated by Indy's very good pass-rush; one sack by Mathis led to a safety, and another sack turned into an interception.

Next, the special teams missed opportunities while also setting up their opponents with excellent field position. Holliday's fumble quickly turned into a touchdown and then he could have scored himself, but was taken down by the kicker.

Finally, it was turnovers—and at crucial times. Hillman's fumble late in the fourth was a nail in the coffin, but Manning's interception set up a score and his sack-fumble turned into two points for Indy. The turnover differential was +2 in favor of the Colts.

While the Broncos were still one of the best teams in the league, these red flags sprung up and showed everyone that they were, in fact, beatable.

Still, at 6-1, the Broncos were in an advantageous position relative to the rest of the league as they started the toughest stretch of their season.

CHAPTER 8

How the West Was Won

> "There's only one way to succeed in anything, and that is to give it everything. I do, and I demand that my players do."
>
> ~ Vince Lombardi

After Denver lost to the Colts, it was a bit of a wakeup call.

It reaffirmed that, yes, they could be beaten. More importantly, it illustrated that when the offense wasn't the greatest thing since the invention of the forward pass, it wasn't enough to support the rest of the team.

Denver's offense was spectacular; the total team product was only so-so, especially minus playmakers on defense and special teams.

The Broncos woke up, alright; when former head coach Mike Shanahan came to town the next week, Denver classily gave him a video montage and standing ovation of his own before they kicked his team's butt and kicked them out of the Mile High City. The 45-21 blowout, in which the defense forced a season-high five turnovers, left everyone on a high going into the bye.

During that usual rest period, something strange—shocking, even—

happened. While playing golf in North Carolina, where John Fox owns an offseason home, the 58-year old felt lightheaded. He was then rushed to an area hospital and given emergency heart valve surgery.

Coaching in the NFL, the millions of dollars and pseudo fame that comes with it, accompanies intense pressure to succeed. It's "win or go home" in the National Football League, it can seem like "life or death." For Fox, that somewhat superficial saying became an all-true reality.

Later, we learned that Fox's doctor saw the faulty valve and that they'd planned on having the surgery after the season. His body couldn't wait.

Much like Derek Wolfe earlier in the year—in that preseason predictor loss to Seattle—Fox was laid-up, on a stretcher, unfit for competition. And just like the eerie sight of Wolfe being put into the back of an ambulance on the field, it seemed impossible. These are our modern day gladiators, men that are asked to and expected to perform more like gods than mere mortals on the gridiron. Fox was their leader; he too, carries the "immortal" label.

The Broncos, though, would be without their calm and cool leader during the most important, most difficult stretch of the schedule.

Luckily for Denver—or, maybe John Elway constructed the team this way on purpose—they had a second head coach on the roster. Just like it was "next man up" on the football field, Fox's backup, defensive coordinator Jack Del Rio, was able to take the reins of the Broncos quickly. His not missing a beat meant the wild stallions were kept in line, not allowed to buck themselves off course.

Well, mostly.

Del Rio is a fiery coach, known for yelling at players and getting under their skin to make them play harder rather than being their friends, like Fox did. Regardless, the Broncos reacted by respecting their interim head coach and playing well for him.

When the team flew to San Diego after the bye, they jumped out to a 21-6 halftime lead by being extremely efficient on offense in the first half. They were sloppier all around in the second, but scored once more—a third Peyton Manning to Demaryius Thomas TD of the game—and held onto win 28-20. Mike McCoy, the offensive coordinator from 2011-12, was the third former Broncos coach to be beaten by the orange and blue that season.

It was a crucial victory for Denver for three reasons; they were back to their winning ways following the bye, it was their second divisional game and it allowed them to pick up a game on the Kansas City Chiefs, who were leading the AFC West at 9-0.

After their bye, the Chiefs—who were the NFL's final unbeaten team of 2013—had to face the 8-1 Broncos at New Mile High.

Kansas City's story was quintessential of the National Football League and its ability to keep fans engaged. The Chiefs went from worst in the league in 2012—they finished a terrible 2-14—to best in the league at the halfway point.

How? By firing their head coach and hiring a new one in Andy Reid, a man that made a living constantly competing in the contentious NFC East. In 14 years as the Philadelphia Eagles' head man, Reid delivered them to the playoffs nine times and led them to the Super Bowl as well.

Reid became a winner by being willing to take risks. He did just that in the 2012 offseason, trading two second round picks (2013, 2014) for former first round quarterback Alex Smith. Smith was the player Kansas City needed. He was a much better quarterback than the team had in recent years. Smith helped bring together an offense that was blessed with multiple talented weapons. Defensively, being bad for multiple years allowed KC to build that side of the ball through the Draft and when 2013 kicked off, many in the media thought the Arrowhead Nation would win the west.

More than halfway through the season, Reid, Smith and the Chiefs weren't disappointing. KC was allowing a mere 12.3 points per game at that point, making them the No. 1 defense.

It was a regular season AFC West matchup of the ages, pitting Denver's distinguished offense against the physical defense of the Chiefs. And, a win would mean much either way in terms of divisional standings.

The game was a hard-fought battle, though the Broncos' 10-point lead after the first quarter wouldn't lead you to believe it. Kansas City battled, and it was 17-7 Denver at the half. Montee Ball rushed in a score to the near pylon in the third, and in the fourth, the physicality showed. Wes Welker was sandwiched between two Chiefs defenders at the end of a big gain, leaving the field with "concussion-like symptoms." Those would resurface as the season went on.

Denver held onto win 27-17—scoring twice as much as KC's defense allowed on average—and took the division lead due to the head-to-head win. The Broncos exposed the Chiefs that day as a fraud. Sure, they had improved greatly from the year before, but Kansas City was still not on the elite level that Denver remained at.

Another week, another headline matchup for the Broncos as they had to go to Foxborough and play the New England Patriots.

It was Brady—Manning XIV, with Tom Brady holding the decided 9-3 edge over Peyton. It was Wes Welker heading home to play the team that let him go. It was the Broncos versus the top coach in all of football, Bill Belichick and the Patriots; a rivalry that went in favor of the team from New England.

In fact, this wasn't just a mano-a-mano rivalry, nor was it simply Belichick versus the Broncos; this rivalry goes back to the first game either of these two storied franchises ever competed in. Rewind to 1960; the AFL was created as a challenge to the NFL and its traditional ways. In the inaugural AFL contest, the Denver Broncos beat the Boston Patriots 13-10, at night, with a white football. It was painted white to assist the players in seeing the usually dark-colored pigskin in the darkness. That game kicked off the rivalry.

In the AFL days, Boston led the series 10-8, with the Broncos leading the NFL matchups 20-10. But, in most recent years, it's been almost all Patriots, going 4-0 since 2011. That included the utter domination and humiliation of Tebow's team 45-10 in the playoffs, ending the Mile High

Messiah's run as a national figure and the starting quarterback of a team, any team. Brady and Belichick had the Broncos' number, year-in, year-out, even when Denver signed Manning. They beat the Broncos 31-21 in 2012 by running up a 31-7 lead by running the ball with power.

2013 seemed to be different, though. Not only were the Broncos better than 2012, the Patriots were worse. Brady was still a world-class quarterback—just like his counterpart—but due to injuries and losses in free agency (Welker), he had far fewer weapons to utilize in the passing game.

All of that didn't matter, though. In the minds of Broncos fans, everything looked great on paper, but there was a feeling that Denver couldn't beat the Pats, that Belichick and Brady were too smart and too talented to take down.

It played into one of the biggest and most memorable games of the 2013 NFL season. One of the wackiest, most exciting and entertaining games anyone had ever seen.

Of course, it was much more than one game. It was more than two of the best teams in the NFL playing one another on a wildly windy and cold November night. The weather was reported at 22 degrees at kickoff with a 22 MPH wind, resulting in a wind chill of -6.

Blustery breezes were historically unkind to passing the football; they would be to Peyton Manning again on this night.

But to begin, it was all about the Denver defense. With the Patriots driving, Steven Ridley carried the ball like a loaf of bread and Wesley Woodyard put his helmet on the ball, forcing a fumble that Von Miller picked up and ran with a quickness, 60 yards, into the end zone. 7-0 Broncos. Miller made everyone remember that night what the team missed from him to start the season.

Seemingly energized by the biggest play he had made all season, Miller ran around Patriots tackle Nate Solder and just as he arrived at Brady to chop the ball loose, Derek Wolfe pounded his facemask into Brady's chest. What resulted was a second straight fumble in New England's first two drives and the massive Terrance Knighton picked the ball up and rumbled to the 10. Two plays later, Knowshon Moreno pushed home the touchdown; 14-0 Denver led, a mere six minutes into the contest.

On their next drive, the unthinkable happened for New England; another fumble. This time, LeGarrette Blount took off to the outside, found some running room before Duke Ihenacho annihilated him, and the ball squirted free.

The Broncos took over at New England's 44, but this wasn't Denver's usual offensive attack. Realizing the wind—which gusted into the 50s at times—was too much to pass into, Manning decided to hand the ball off repeatedly. It worked, but only well enough to move into field goal range; 17-0 Denver.

Another drive, another turnover by New England. This time, just a punt, though.

When Denver got the ball back, it was much of the same. Moreno ran relentlessly and Manning tried to pass for short gains, getting lucky as Montee Ball picked up 31 yards after a short completion. Facing a 3rd and 5 from the Patriots' 10, Manning threw his best ball of the game, up the seam and in-stride to Jacob Tamme for the touchdown. 24-0 Broncos at the half.

Broncos fans rejoiced; they were finally going to beat Belichick, Brady and the hated Patriots!

Not so fast.

The Patriots were electric—possibly set on fire by Belichick in the locker room—and came out swinging. Brady led a quick touchdown drive, finding Welker's replacement, Danny Amendola, in the back corner of the end zone; 24-7 Denver.

On the next Denver drive, a screen pass to Ball turned into a fumble and the Pats capitalized with a Brandon Bolden touchdown run. The Broncos still led, though, 24-14.

Denver tried to finally come out in their usual shotgun formation offense, but on 3rd and 5, Manning fumbled the ball to force a punt and give possession back to the Patriots.

"Uh-oh" time for the Broncos..

Brady got comfortable and found Julian Edelman for a 34-yard gain, which set up a laser from the quarterbacking great to massive tight end Rob Gronkowski. 24-21, Denver, with mere seconds remaining in the third quarter.

Three plays later, Manning stared down Eric Decker and still threw it to him—off his back foot, nonetheless—which resulted in an interception. We—a national television audience—were witnessing one of the biggest choke jobs, one of the most massive collapses in a long time. 24-point halftime leads aren't surmounted every week, in fact, you have to go back to 2012 and Denver's comeback over the Chargers to find a similar situation. Sickening for Broncos fans.

That's because, three plays following Manning's interception was a touchdown pass from Brady to Edelman. Not only had Denver's 24-point lead evaporated, they were now trailing 28-24. And for the greatest offense anyone had ever seen, it seemed Manning and his men had forgotten how to score. Hell, they'd forgotten how to pick up a first down. Denver went three-and-out on their next drive.

But Brady knew it wouldn't be enough, which is why his dynamic drive resulted in even more points, this time a 31-yard field goal by Stephen Gostkowski. That was after Woodyard missed a should-be interception and Brady slightly overthrew Amendola in the end zone. Most games have one turning point, this contest had the potential for a multitude of them. Still, five straight scores for the Pats, 31 unanswered points and it was 31-24 New England with 7:37 to play.

Finally, and almost out of nowhere, Manning and the offense showed life for the first time all half. The wind and cold seemed to freeze their ability to execute, until the game was on the line. On one crucial 3rd and 5, Manning gunned a pass into a covered Tamme for a first down. Then, with time ticking down, the Sheriff floated one in stride to Demaryius Thomas for a score up the sideline. We were all tied up at 31.

And for the first time in the 47-game history of the rivalry, it went into overtime. The wind actually got worse as the game went on, making it almost impossible to pass. Neither team could move the ball, punting possession back and forth four times.

Then it happened.

The nearly four-hour long contest that was filled with drama, ended somewhat anticlimactically.

With just north of three minutes to go, Ryan Allen punted away to Wes Welker, who backed away from the ball while giving teammates the "poison" call. Backup cornerback Tony Carter didn't listen though, and ran mindlessly into the ball's path, where it careened off him and found its way into the awaiting arms of Nate Ebner of New England. Three plays later, Gostkowski kicked home the game-winner, 31 yards, for the 34-31 victory.

It was a devastating loss, after being up so big—24 points—at halftime. It wasn't just that Manning and the offense had a field day like most weeks. It was the defense that propelled the offense for the first time all season long. But they couldn't capitalize, and all that effort, all that extraordinary play by Miller and the others was for not.

The Broncos had squandered a massive opportunity to beat one of their rivals on the road and couldn't get the job done.

Denver dropped to 9-2, while New England improved to 8-3. It tightened up the race for the No. 1 seed, and if the Broncos tied with the Pats, New England would have home-field advantage.

If the Broncos could rebound the next week, though, it'd be all good.

That's because, unusually, they played the Chiefs for the second time in the season in a mere three weeks.

Before the game, Knowshon Moreno—who had grown into the role of Broncos' emotional leader, was shown on the sideline, crying tears so large they would flood a small car—he wasn't the only player on the team who was charged to play the Chiefs.

That game was all about Peyton Manning and Eric Decker. Unlike the game in Foxborough, Arrowhead's weather was much more pleasant.

Manning was able to throw the ball with ease and enjoyed a five passing touchdown day.

Four of the scores went to Decker, a record in its own right.

To start, the Chiefs offense worked like a well-tuned instrument, moving the ball downfield with ease. But on a first and goal from the three, Alex Smith rolled out and threw the ball without enough arc; Wesley Woodyard jumped in and stole the interception in the end zone. Momentum killer.

Manning answered with an interception of his own, though, as a deep ball to Demaryius Thomas bounced off the receiver's hands as he was bustled by two Chiefs defensive backs. Not only did Quintin Demps pick off Peyton, Thomas injured his shoulder on the play. The effects would linger deep into the playoffs.

Kansas City capitalized on the turnover, turning it into a touchdown pass from Smith to J. Hemingway for the 7-0 lead.

To start the second quarter, Manning cocked back and slung a deep pass down the middle of the field to Eric Decker as he split two defenders; tied game.

The positive play on offense was immediately countered with yet another special teams blunder, which seemed to happen every single Sunday. The Matt Prater kickoff sailed eight yards into the end zone, but teams knew by then that yards were there for the taking on kicks; Knile Davis ran it out, ran past a group of Broncos that were stymied by blocks, jetted away from a few more and to the house. The 108-yard play was the longest in the history of Kansas City's football franchise. Embarrassing. 14-7 Chiefs. To make matters worse, Manning threw woefully short and was picked off for a second time mere plays later, and Smith took his team 22 yards into the Broncos end zone to widen their lead to 21-7.

Later in the quarter, No. 18 slung a deep one, on the money to Decker, moving the team into scoring range. Moreno caught a pass out of the backfield and lowered his shoulder into the end zone. 21-14 Chiefs, end of the half.

To start the second half, Manning went for the massive play and connected; Decker ran away from his cornerback and the safety, his quarterback put the ball on the money and the 37-yard pass tied the game up at 21. New ballgame.

Sensing the shift in momentum, Denver's defense forced a punt and when he got the ball back, Manning saw an opening, quickly sending a signal to Thomas that told him to run a go route. He caught the ball and ran for 77 yards, to the Chiefs' 15. From there, Decker caught the touchdown on a post pattern, giving Denver their first lead of the pivotal contest.

The Broncos got the ball back quickly and Montee Ball rumbled to midfield, 45 yards with power and acceleration. A few plays later, Decker ran a corner fade, a perfect pass by Peyton extended the lead to 35-21 early in the fourth quarter.

Kansas City wouldn't quit—knowing their hopes of winning the AFC West were on the line—and their epic, 17-play drive was capped by a Jamaal Charles touchdown plunge. 35-28 Denver, 6:32 left to play.

This is where Manning's magnificence would shine, the Broncos would milk the clock and win, right? Not exactly. The orange and blue mixed runs with deep passes to run the clock, and a huge play by Moreno almost guaranteed a win.

With the game on the line and Denver in position to put it away, Moreno caught a short pass out of the backfield, ran through first contact, continued to run while four Chiefs players attempted to gang-tackle him and after the referees blew the play dead, decided to army crawl on the ground, finally signaling a first down from his belly. On a team that was still feeling itself out with the more reserved Manning as their leader, Moreno provided that raw spark that got everyone going. No, it wasn't just that Moreno had finally lived up to his potential in this, his fifth season in the league, nor that he had developed into a coveted weapon as a multi-faceted running back; Moreno provided the intangible of emotional leader, too.

But that first down wasn't enough; the Chiefs called their second timeout and incomplete passes led to a punt back to K.C. with 3:32 to go.

This is where the Chiefs—and Alex Smith—would choke, right? It seemed that way. A hold on 2nd and 8 pushed the team back to their four yard line, in the shadow of their own end zone, needing a touchdown. Multiple deep passes—of 26, 28 and 23 yards—moved the team into the red zone with a quickness, though. After the two minute warning, K.C. was 17 yards away, facing a 3rd and 8. Smith's short pass netted four yards, but left them with a 4th and 4 which would decide the game. On that crucial play, Smith went for it all, throwing the pigskin up to Dwayne Bowe in the end zone, where Broncos safety Mike Adams knocked it down to secure a victory for Denver.

The win meant a stranglehold on the AFC West. As Denver improved to 10-2, the Chiefs fell to 9-3 and the Broncos owned both head-to-head matches.

How was the West was won? In dominant fashion by the Denver Broncos.

As for Jack Del Rio, he did as well as anyone could have hoped considering the circumstances. 3-1 was stellar, his leadership was strong and the team never lost a beat. He must be commended, and it was also during this time that JDR was rumored to be in the running as the University of Southern California's head coaching position. Teaching, preparing and competing through adversity and distractions is what this team was made of; it almost took them to the summit of the NFL.

But, it'd still be a fight down the final stretch if the Broncos wanted to clinch that coveted No. 1 seed and the home-field advantage that accompanied it.

CHAPTER 9

REGULAR SEASON HOME STRETCH, RECORD-SETTING STYLE

> *"Leaders are made, they are not born. They are made by hard effort, which is the price which all of us must pay to achieve any goal that is worthwhile."*
> ~ *Vince Lombardi*

After their emotional win over the Chiefs to take a commanding AFC West lead, Denver made sure to continue the momentum. They wanted to crush their next opponent, the Tennessee Titans, which is exactly what they did.

But in the week before the game, all the talk focused on Peyton Manning's inability to perform at his usual mile high level in cold-weather games because the forecast called for a chilly mid-December day. To that point, Manning had been a mere 3-7 in games in which the temperature at kickoff was 32 degrees or lower, leading many football analysts to draw the conclusion that he couldn't win cold-weather contests.

Even without a headline opponent—the Titans were a mediocre team at best when they came to the Mile High City—there were plenty of headlines surrounding the Broncos.

Adding to the noise were the two standout losses which had already occurred during Manning's short time in Denver. The most crucial failure was the home playoff loss to the Ravens. Any time the specter of a cold-weather game is conjured, fans have flashbacks of this loss, one of the worst collapses anyone who bleeds orange and blue can remember. And even more recent was the overtime loss in New England only two weeks before, which had the feeling of a playoff game. Denver led 24-0 before allowing Tom Brady and the Patriots to come all the way back and even take the lead. Manning's last-second drive tied it up, but then a gaffe in the waning seconds by Denver's special teams gave the game away.

Understandably, people in the media and die-hard Broncos backers were suspect of Manning's ability to perform in the chilly weather. On this Sunday afternoon, he made it appear as if he wanted to silence all the critics.

Believe me, it was cold. So cold, in fact, I had the ability to purchase two tickets the day before the game and couldn't find anyone willing to brave the cold. I asked a longtime family friend and a Titans fan. No go. Three other Denver "die-hards"—more like fair-weather fans, literally—chickened out and I had to watch from the comfort of my couch. And at the beginning of the game, I was happy to be inside, sheltered from the 18 degree weather (11 degrees with the wind chill) as Tennessee came to play.

Despite their poor record (5-7) and the cold, the Titans were fighting to win. Tennessee jumped out to a 7-0 lead when Shonn Greene pounded the ball between the tackles, and the Broncos answered with a methodical drive capped off by a 4rd and 1 pass from Manning to Wes Welker to tie it up. But then the special teams let the rest of their teammates down for a third straight week, allowing Leon Washington—known as an electrifying kick returner—to take Matt Prater's kickoff 95 yards to the Denver three yard line. The very next play, Chris Johnson pushed the ball over the goal line for the 14-7 lead.

The Titans were making it look way too easy to score as both the special teams and defensive units of Denver lacked luster at the onset of play.

After exchanging punts, Peyton transitioned to the no-huddle offense, which worked wonderfully. Manning mixed up short and long passes as well as his receivers, and on the drive's fifth play, his beautifully thrown ball hit Eric Decker in stride for the touchdown. The replay evidence, however, betrayed the receiver. Decker was touched down just short of the goal line, at the two—no touchdown. Following a false start three plays later, Manning hit Welker for another touchdown fated to be reversed by the replay official. The Broncos eventually had to settle for a 25-yard field goal, squandering an opportunity to tie the game. They remained down 10-14.

A punt by Britton Colquitt pinned Tennessee all the way back at the 11 and three straight runs by Greene resulted in a first down. On the next play, Von Miller fought his way through a block to get to Fitzpatrick, who threw incomplete. At the end of the play, Miller's helmet struck the quarterback's facemask; it was a personal foul and an automatic first down. Three plays later, Fitzpatrick hit Nate Washington for a gain of eight yards near midfield. Tennessee decided to go for it on 4th and 2. The Broncos weren't ready and had to call their first timeout of the half. When the Titans took the field again, they converted on a short pass to Chris Johnson which went 23 yards. On the very next play Greene took the ball 28 yards off left tackle and Tennessee led 21-10.

This was anything but expected between two teams at opposite ends of the NFL spectrum. For Denver, this was supposed to be a tune-up game.

Manning, again in the no-huddle, regained his mastery. He went 7-8 on this particular drive, throwing passes short, medium and long—a beauty went for 30 yards to Welker up the seam—to move his team deep into enemy territory. From the eight yard line, he found Julius Thomas on a fade route and the tight end athletically tippy-toed both feet for the TD. Tennessee was still in the lead 21-17.

With a mere 51 seconds left in the half, Denver found themselves with the ball once again—and the same score. They started at their own 10. A pass interference penalty on Tennessee combined with passes to

Demaryius Thomas and Decker pushed the team to the Titans' 46 yard line with three seconds to play. That is when history was made.

Matt Prater, well-known as one of the biggest legs in all of football, stepped up and drilled a 64-yard field goal as time ran out. It was all the more impressive due to the very cold weather—18 degrees at kickoff—which can hurt a football's hang-time due to the heavier air. Prater celebrated crazily with teammates, fist-pumping and banging his helmet on the ever emotional Knowshon Moreno's; he was feeling the exuberance of breaking an NFL record.

That kick left the entirety of Sports Authority Field at Mile High Stadium abuzz as the half ended. Bronco fans—known for being well-informed—understood they'd just witnessed history.

And really, when you sit back and watch sports, isn't that the best part of it all? Watching history being made on live television, even better yet, in person, is simply awe-inspiring. To think, this particular feat you just witnessed never before happened in the 94 years of the National Football League is enough to elicit goose bumps, to send adrenaline coursing through your veins.

Without a doubt, that kick was the turning point of the game. If Prater had missed, it would have been an "oh well" type of situation. But it visibly pumped up the crowd and pumped up the team. Tennessee was living up to the hype; in the NFL, no team will simply roll over and die, even when they know the playoffs are out of reach. Every game matters in the NFL and when you're a team as dominant as Denver, you get every opponent's A-game, each and every week.

The Broncos bolted out of the locker room and into the no-huddle; their most effective way of attack since it disallowed time to make changes for defenses. Manning hit Demaryius Thomas down the right sideline for 38 yards to the Tennessee four. On the very next play, Thomas was the recipient of a touchdown pass and the Broncos' first lead of the day, 27-21.

That drive was a microcosm of the second half, in which Denver was able to do anything and everything they wanted. Moreno and Ball ran with toughness, Manning picked apart the Titan defense with ease and even the Denver D showed glimpses of its scary 2012 self. On one play in particular, Von Miller's relentless pursuit caused star running back Chris Johnson to turn 360 degrees in search of an open lane, only to then have Miller force a fumble that Mike Adams recovered.

When it was all said and done, Ball punched home the final touchdown for the 51-28 victory, the third 50-plus point scoring output by the Broncos on the season.

Right after the final touchdown, CBS's television cameras showed John Elway on the sidelines, chuckling as his masterfully constructed Broncos made the Titans look like the laughing stock of the league. His look was the definition of confidence, which is what the team represented at that very moment. That almost cocky attitude would eventually haunt them, but for this week, Elway and his Broncos were the kings of the NFL. Not only was Peyton proficient with a glove on in the cold—going 39-59 for 397 yards and four scores—but the defense had regained its pass-rushing prowess.

A residual kind of cockiness lasted during the short week of preparation before the Thursday night contest against the Chargers. The Broncos were basically on cruise control. They rolled team after team all season long, and even on a short week, didn't lack any confidence.

During practice, the defensive linemen lined up and ran pass routes, catching throws during the short lead-up to the game. Maybe it was all in good fun following Terrance Knighton's interception the week before—letting the big men show off their skills—but it may not have been what the team should have been focusing on. When does a defensive lineman ever go out for a pass in a game? Instead, they should have been focusing on using their hands to shed blocks in order to put pressure on the quarterback and tackle ball-carriers. Along those same lines, coaches John Fox and Jack Del Rio started experimenting on defense, which was silly, to say the least. The defense was certainly the team's weakness. Benching Wesley Woodyard as well as Duke Ihenacho represented questionable and perhaps frivolous decision making.

As the game drew closer, the team reeked of complacency; they had already clinched a playoff berth four days earlier and in their own eyes, had already won the AFC.

Then, a hungry and hanging-on-by-the-skin-of-their-teeth San Diego Chargers team gave the Broncos a distressing drubbing. Or, made them look like donkeys, if you will. And they did so in the Mile High finale, to boot.

Denver started strong and scored a quick touchdown on their first drive. Manning was magical as always, connecting with Andre Caldwell in the front left corner of the end zone for the 7-0 lead. After San Diego's first drive resulted in a field goal, Denver drove down again, only to fall short of the end zone and have Matt Prater kick a 32-yarder for the 10-3 lead.

The Chargers caught fire and the Broncos stunk like a dumpster fire. Denver went three-and-out three times to finish the first half, while San Diego—led by Philip Rivers—stormed ahead for the 17-10 lead. Rivers tossed two touchdowns to rookie receiver Keenan Allen, each were remarkable plays. On the first, Allen took the ball at the 10 yard line, turned up field for positive yardage and leapt over cornerback Kayvon Webster, then floated in the air to the one and his forward momentum carried Allen through Mike Adams for the score. The second was a beautifully thrown pass from Rivers to the same front left corner of the end zone Denver scored in on their first drive, as it went through Webster's hands and somehow into Allen's. He held on through the contact with the ground and scored magnificently.

In the second half, both sides of the ball continued to struggle mightily for Denver as they were called for multiple 12 men on the field penalties, had to burn two timeouts due to poor preparedness and a critical neutral zone infraction cost the team dearly. After they made San Diego punt from their own end zone, Nate Webster jumped off sides and handed the Chargers a first down which they transformed into a long and meticulous drive. By the time a Ryan Mathews score put the Chargers ahead by a score of 24-10 late in the third quarter, seven minutes had been milked off the clock.

Finally, Manning willed his team to action. They put together a structured 12-play drive for 89 yards and a touchdown that ended when Manning hit Caldwell for another TD. With over six minutes to play and down only one TD, the team had life. But the defense allowed San Diego to work the clock, although they eventually forced a punt. The Broncos had that brief spark of life extinguished when Manning was intercepted soon thereafter. His late pick set up a 35-yard field goal by Nick Novak and basically bankrupted any hope of victory. A quick field goal drive by Denver made it a touchdown game, again, but it was too little, too late. A too-short onside kick by Prater meant the game was over.

The loss was troubling for a multitude of reasons.

First and foremost, it meant the Broncos fell to 11-3, just a half-game ahead of the New England Patriots in the conference and one game ahead of the Kansas City Chiefs in the division. Beyond that, it was the Broncos' first divisional loss of the season and their first to an AFC West foe since Manning joined the team in early 2012.

They were the team with all the answers early. Now, there were only question marks.

One of the biggest glaring questions surrounded the deficient defense which threatened to bring the entire season down with its putrid play. While Woodyard played more than he had in the previous game, Paris Lenon still made multiple glaring mistakes. Woodyard was this team's defensive leader, making the move from weakside to middle linebacker in the weeks leading up to the season, which is much more difficult a task than the five-year captain let on. He was the voice in the defensive huddle all season, their unifying piece in a fractured puzzle with far too many holes due to a myriad of injuries. He was a consummate professional, a six-time captain for the team. Without Woodyard, the defense was done. The Week 5 barn-burner inside "Jerry World" proved as much. Yet coaches rested (benched) him.

Duke Ihenacho—a young, playmaking safety who answered the call and stepped up into a larger role—also played, but it was Webster who was picked on over and over again by Rivers. The run defense was nonexistent with 177 yards allowed and the pass-rush also failed to materialize with only two sacks.

To make matters worse, things got out of control after the loss.

Following the game, four people were stabbed in a private parking lot adjacent to Sports Authority Field at Mile High Stadium. This followed a stabbing in the parking lot of Arrowhead Stadium after the Broncos beat the Chiefs in their home. While there have always been fights—especially between fans of AFC West rivals and Broncos fans in Denver—stabbings were thought to be a rare occurrence. These events are uncalled for, unacceptable and unfortunate.

In the days after the loss, many Broncos fans started believing the sky was falling, the season was over and that the men from the Mile High City didn't deserve to win a Super Bowl. This was one loss—one regular season loss—but fans were distraught. Of course, it was a tough loss to a hated rival in Rivers and the Chargers—everything added up to a perfect storm of disappointment. It wasn't just that the defense let the group down; the Broncos' special teams unit was again suspect and even the offense struggled.

Once a seemingly unbeatable team, the Broncos were found to be mortal in their loss to the Colts in Indy, but that could be explained away. More cracks developed in the loss to New England, however; it was this game which brought the Broncos' championship chops into question. There was no way they could win a Super Bowl with the defense and special teams that were on display in the second half of the season.

Even the offense wasn't itself. Notably, Wes Welker sat out of the contest due to a concussion. While this opened the door for Bubba Caldwell's biggest day as a Bronco, it didn't equal the usual profound production. Welker is a go-to guy on third downs, simple as that. When Manning didn't have him, the offense went three-and-out three straight times to end the first half. To this point, Welker led the team with 18 catches on third downs for an average of 11.4 yards per reception; his absence was obvious as the Broncos went a putrid 2-9 on the all-important third down conversions.

Another pronounced problem for the offense was the complete ineptitude by the rushing attack. Denver ran the ball a mere 11 times for a total of 18 yards; by far their worst performance on the ground all year. That lack of balance allowed San Diego to lock in on receivers. Welker's injury and the team's inability to find open space on option routes meant Denver couldn't light up the scoreboard like they wanted to.

After two days of sulking and seeing the sky fall down on Bronco Country, Sunday brought good news. Denver had to have the Miami Dolphins beat the New England Patriots to regain the No. 1 seed in the AFC. The chances seemed slim, as Miami wasn't near the equal of the Patriots, at least, on paper. But similar to San Diego, the Dolphins needed to win to keep their own playoff hopes alive. Desperate teams are determined teams, and somehow, some way, the desperate Dolphins won 24-20 over Tom Brady and the Pats.

The playoff implications were massive. First and foremost, it meant the Broncos were back in the drivers' seat of the American Football Conference. Without a doubt, avoiding playing in Foxborough—where it's likely to be bitterly cold in January—was a big deal to Manning and Denver. Yes, the game against Tennessee was in the cold, but that only brought Manning's cold-weather game numbers up to 4-7 overall, 0-3 while in New England in the playoffs. The Pats loss to Miami also meant that, with a win, the Cincinnati Bengals could move up to that No. 2 seed dropping New England to third. That was not fated to be as the Bengals played terribly, falling prey to the steel curtain of their division foe Pittsburgh Steelers at a frigid Heinz Field.

When Week 15 was all said and done, the Broncos were still No. 1, at 11-3.

The cherry on top was Peyton Manning's honor. It was announced late that Sunday night that Manning earned *Sports Illustrated* Sportsman of the Year, one of the few major, national awards he had yet to receive up to this point in his storied career. In the amazingly well-written piece by Lee Jenkins, it wasn't all about Manning's mastery of the football field, but how he got there. We all knew the man loved to study, but the way Jenkins' piece goes into detail about those superior study habits provides us with a glimpse of Manning's intense focus. One equipment man said the quarterback invited him in to watch film. For an hour they looked at one play, back and forth, back and forth. The equipment guy admitted to nodding off, never finding out if the play was even a run or a pass. Jenkins also talked about the innumerable handwritten, tear-jerking letters Manning handed out over the years to players, coaches and even fans.

He was without a doubt the best quarterback in the league in 2013, but this honor was about much more than that. Sure, Manning's a multitalented man. He moonlights as the pitch man for Papa John's Pizza, Buick and others as well as being a funny guy on *Saturday Night Live*. Fans were given a unique behind-the-scenes illustration of who the quarterbacking legend is. If you're a fan of the Broncos, Peyton Manning or football in general, I strongly encourage you go out find a copy of the magazine or read the lengthy feature on SI.com.

With their third loss of the season still burning the Broncos, a matchup with the worst team in football, the Houston Texans, awaited them. To add a little something extra—as was the case this entire season—Denver was playing against one of their former coaches, Wade Phillips. Phillips was the head coach in the Mile High City in from 1993-94, before the Mike Shanahan Era, going a mediocre 16-16. Phillips was the third current head coach to face his former team this season, and wildly, he replaced Gary Kubiak, who was not only John Elway's offensive coordinator, but his backup quarterback and even training camp roommate at one time. Kubiak was fired by Houston following a terrible 2-11 start; not even a stroke on the sideline earlier in the season could save his job. The NFL can be a ruthless place.

And on this Sunday morning, the Broncos didn't pull any punches.

The Houston Texans were 2-12 when 11-3 Denver came to town; this was seemingly the perfect matchup to bounce back from a loss with a dominating win. What the team forgot, though, was that their opponents get paid too. The Texans fought with all their heart and made it a game in the second half before the Broncos caught fire.

The game began slowly, with each team exchanging field goals. After moving his team to the Houston 36, the first quarter ended, and when the game came back from the break, Peyton Manning unleashed a deep pass that hit Demaryius Thomas in stride for the first touchdown of the day.

Houston forced the Broncos to punt on their next drive and Keshawn Martin exposed their special teams. He returned a punt 51 yards to the Denver 33, setting up the Texans offense with wonderful field position. Matt Schaub handed it off to rookie Dennis Johnson four times in a row and then threw it to him once to set up a 3rd and 11. On that third and long, Schaub looked for talented receiver Andre Johnson but missed him, setting up Randy Bullock with a 35-yard field goal that he drilled.

With 6:06 left in the first half, the Broncos went to work. This was one of those masterful drives in which Manning mixed in the run with the pass to keep the opposing defense off balance. The quarterback spread the ball around, but that 13-play drive merely resulted in a short field goal by Matt Prater, not what Denver wanted.

Still, after the defense forced a quick three-and-out, Manning threw to Decker, Julius Thomas and then Jacob Tamme to set up a 44-yard field goal, giving the team a 16-6 halftime lead.

The Broncos opened the second half with a three-and-out and Houston took advantage of the good fortune. On 3rd and 3, Schaub found Ryan Griffin scampering free on a corner route. The tight end secured the ball and turned up the sidelines for many more yards, 40 in all. A couple plays later, Schaub rolled out to the right, searched for an open receiver and then saw Martin running across the back of the end zone; Houston's QB put great touch on the ball to deliver it high over Kayvon Webster's hand and into Martin's arms. That score brought the game to 16-13 Denver, and people started to panic.

Without a doubt, the Texans had stolen the momentum at this point. Fans on Twitter started saying things like, "This isn't a Super Bowl team," and, "The Broncos are going the wrong way heading into the playoffs..." and so on. Poor play fed those fears as the once unstoppable offense went three-and-out two more times.

That's when the Denver defense finally stepped up. After Britton Colquitt's third straight punt of the half, Robert Ayers rushed, sacked and forced Schaub to fumble. The Texans recovered but Schaub was sacked the very next play by Danny Trevathan as Jack Del Rio astutely called a blitz on 3rd and 12.

As it turned out, Schaub wasn't the only one feeling the heat of the opposing defense. On Denver's next drive, Manning was hit in the ribs by J.J. Watt, who forced the veteran quarterback to throw the ball off his back foot; it floated in the air and fell a few yards away from Julius Thomas, who had come open too late. Watt—one of the most feared pass-rushers in the NFL—not only hit Manning in the ribs, the 6'5", 289-pound lineman also drove the 37-year old QB into the turf. It could have been called a personal foul, but wasn't and Manning got up a little gingerly before trotting to the sideline, his team up by a narrow margin of only three points as the third quarter expired.

But when that game-deciding fourth quarter began, we once again saw how important having an elite quarterback can be. On second down, Schaub dropped back and the Denver defensive line busted through. Specifically, Shaun Phillips came around the right side of the line while Terrance Knighton knifed through two Houston blockers. It caused Schaub to roll to his right as both big men chased him towards the Houston sideline and then, instead of taking the sack that would have resulted in a major loss of yards, the Texans quarterback tried to fit the ball into Martin on the sideline. Instead, safety Mike Adams made a terrific play, jumping in front of the receiver and intercepting the pass while tapping his toes to get his feet inbounds.

On the next play, Knowshon Moreno ran right for 18 yards, setting up a first-and-goal from the 10. Manning found Decker open on a 5-yard slant. The receiver walked in for the score and spiked the ball with such a fury it bounced 10 yards in the air. 23-13 Broncos.

Adams' interception proved to be the turning point and the Broncos controlled the rest of the game. Houston had to punt the ball once again and Manning answered with a beautifully thrown touchdown pass to Decker. Cornerback Kareem Jackson was blanketing Decker, but Manning still dropped the ball perfectly into his receiver's awaiting hands. That touchdown gave Denver the 30-13 lead and was Manning's 50th TD of the season, only the second time the feat had been accomplished.

Yet another punt from the Texans set Manning up with the ability to throw his record-setting 51st touchdown of the season. The play was strikingly similar to Decker's second touchdown, but on the opposite side of the field, and to Julius Thomas. Thomas, the tight end, lined up wide to the right and the Houston defense put a linebacker on him; it was a mismatch Manning was likely drooling over when the ball was snapped. Thomas ran a fly near the Broncos' sideline and Manning put the ball on him in stride, allowing "Orange Julius" to cruise into the near corner for the record-setting score and the 37-13 lead.

After the touchdown pass, Manning trotted down to the end zone and was met with high fives and head pats from all of his teammates. In fact, the game was stopped for a minute, allowing Manning to squeeze out of his helmet and wave to the Houston crowd, who showed a lot of class and gave the legend a standing ovation. When he got to the sideline, Jack Del Rio—a former fearsome linebacker and fiery defensive coordinator—rubbed his head and hair much like a proud parent would do to a child after winning an award or accomplishing a goal; it was a cool, unique moment. While football is surrounded by macho men and a machismo culture, this was a sweet, heartwarming instant. Also, not something NFL fans see every week, or even every year.

The win meant the Broncos improved to 12-3 on the season and clinched their AFC West division for the third straight year. It wasn't a perfectly executed game—the offense went three-and-out four times and the defense was so-so at best—but it was a win on the road in December, one Denver needed to keep their hold on the AFC's top seed.

The Broncos final regular season game meant flying to Oakland to battle their hated division rivals, the Raiders. Oakland entered the contest 4-11, with former Broncos defensive coordinator Dennis Allen sitting squarely on the hot seat as his second season head coaching the men in black and silver came to a close.

Allen and his Rai-duhs—a nickname given to the team that has endured 10 straight losing seasons since last going to the Super Bowl in January of 2003—were without a doubt no match for Denver's record-setting offense. Even Peyton Manning and Co. couldn't get the fans out of their houses in Oakland as the entire top deck of the Coliseum was tarped over; the bottom deck wasn't much better, lightly speckled with spectators.

In reality, it made Raiders fans look smart for staying home as the Broncos put on a football clinic. Those Oakland players weren't smart enough to catch onto the lessons.

To start the game, Denver's defense forced a quick three-and-out and were more energetic than in recent weeks. Manning immediately took his team down field by dumping the ball to Knowshon Moreno on short passes, eventually connecting with Eric Decker on a pivot route for the first score of the day.

On the Raiders' very next offensive play, a poor snap hit quarterback Terrelle Pryor in the left hip and bounced to the ground. Sylvester Williams pounced and the ball was back in Bronco possession. Four plays later, Manning dumped it again to Moreno, who turned up-field for the touchdown and 14-0 lead. The rout was on.

After the Oakland offense floundered again, they gave the ball back to Manning and his merry men. A lengthy drive ended when a sack on the Raiders 16 by Lamarr Houston made Denver line up and kick a successful

34-yard field goal. On their next possession, Manning enjoyed his most beautiful pass of the day. The bomb floated in the air and fell into the fingertips of a speeding Demaryius Thomas, allowing the freakishly fast receiver to blaze into the end zone for the 24-0 lead.

If the Raiders still had hopes of winning, they were dashed the minute Thomas darted to pay-dirt.

Oakland managed to pick up a first down on their next series, but punted four plays later, giving the Broncos just over three minutes to score a nail-in-the-coffin TD. As with most of the drives in the first half, short passes ruled as Manning and his receivers took what they could get with low-risk throws. On a first and goal from the five yard line, Manning made it look to easy as he threw a short out to Thomas and the receiver stretched the ball across the goal line. That play resulted in Manning's 55th touchdown of the season, as well as being just enough—by one yard—to earn the passing yards in a season record (5,477). The play pushed the Broncos lead to 31-0.

The end of the half drive was perfectly executed; the Broncos didn't even face a third down while running out nearly all of the time and scoring a touchdown before the break. In fact, the entire first half was nearly perfectly executed by the offense; five drives resulted in five scores, with one stall turning into a Prater field goal.

What can't be missed is the supreme play by the defense in the first half. While Terrelle Pryor was a first-year starter in 2013, his 6-11 passing for 35 yards at halftime had some to do with Denver's D. They pressured him well while sticking with receivers, forcing Pryor to try and find yards on the ground. Here's a way to encapsulate the utter dominance by Denver in the first half; while the Broncos scored on all five of their drives, the Raiders' possessions looked like this: punt, fumble, punt, punt, punt, half.

Hands down, it was the most dominant Denver play of the season, on both offense and defense. For all intents and purposes, the game was over at halftime. Manning was pulled, giving way to second-year backup Brock Osweiler, who controlled the ball and controlled the clock by running the rock. Denver dominated to win 34-14.

With the victory, the Broncos improved to 13-3 and earned the AFC's No. 1 seed for the second straight season. The Broncos ended the season on a high note in all three phases and looked every bit the Super Bowl contender they were built to be.

The 2013 Broncos are the No. 1 offense of all time, scoring 606 points, 76 touchdowns 5,562 passing yards, 56 passing touchdowns...these are all NFL records.

This was Denver's time to shine, their year to win it all.

Wasn't it?

CHAPTER 10

RIDING THE MOMENTUM

> *"We shall play every game to the hilt with every ounce of fiber we have in our bodies"*
>
> ~ *Vince Lombardi*

Before the Broncos could do anything to prepare for their next opponent, "Black Monday" kicked off the week.

The day after the regular season ended, five teams fired their head coaches, including the Washington Redskins who parted ways with former Broncos coaching great Mike Shanahan.

In turn, those vacancies meant five teams were looking to fill head coaching positions; Denver possessed two of the most highly coveted coordinators around. Both Adam Gase and Jack Del Rio were viewed as potential candidates. For Gase, it was the Cleveland Browns and Minesota Vikings who came calling. In Del Rio's case, it was also the Vikings—where he played linebacker professionally in the 1980s—who were interested in his services. Gase told both the Browns and Vikings he wouldn't interview until the Broncos' season was over, while the Del Rio to Minnesota talks may have been nothing more than rumors.

Gase running the offense in Denver meant he was a big-time acquisition in many teams' eyes. His talent was unquestioned—promoting him to offensive coordinator from quarterback's coach was one of the first things John Elway did in 2013.

So while it may have been a much-deserved and earned bye week, it didn't bring too much rest for the Broncos. According to Head Coach John Fox, the team took Monday through Wednesday off, a smart move as everyone in the league has bumps and bruises by the time 17 weeks of war on the gridiron has come and gone. Players needed rest, and three days seemed like just enough, but not too much.

Coach Fox famously called it a "get better week" not a bye week.

"It's about preparation," he said on Thursday, following the team's first postseason practice. "One of the reasons why you work hard to get to this situation is that it gives you an extra week to prepare for a potential opponent. You don't know exactly but our guys had a good workout today. There was good focus and this is an opportunity to get better. A lot of people on the outside call it a 'bye' week. To me it's a 'get better' week."

During the Elway-Manning Era, led by two of the most competitive NFL personalities in history, the goal was to constantly improve. The legendary concept, Kaizen, based on the Japanese word "kaizen" (or, 'happy change"), basically means the striving toward continual improvement in any process. There was no time to completely rest, the Broncos were trying to win a Super Bowl. Kaizen was happening, everywhere.

That same day, Manning was asked if losing the season before in the playoffs' Divisional round helped better prepare the Broncos this time. "Like I said, I think you can—as painful as it was—I think you can learn from it," Manning explained. "I think you can use it certainly to fuel you. But you can learn from some of the situational football parts of it. I think you can learn from 16 more games this regular season. It was a new team last year. It's still a new team this year but there is more familiarity and hopefully we have more chemistry with the players that have been on both teams. The players that are new this year, I think we've been through a lot here in just 16 games and hopefully that can help us."

The quote shines a little light into what Manning—and likely his teammates—were thinking all along, in both 2012 and 2013. In 2012, it was a brand new team, one led by Manning. He had to adapt to playing in Denver with all his new teammates just as much as they had to adapt to Peyton the perfectionist in film study, on the practice field and then out in front of the crowd at New Mile High stadium. There were expectations in 2012, sure, but not like the ones in his second season. In Peyton's eyes, it's about taking all that experience to create chemistry and also learn from it all, then applying that newfound knowledge in the playoffs.

Leading up to Wild Card weekend, I wanted to take a closer statistical look at the situation and the Broncos' well earned "get better" week. After doing the research, I wrote a column to share my findings. Published on *Cover32* and reprinted below, the numbers spun more of a cautionary tale than one may have expected.

Is first round bye a curse in disguise for Broncos?

While four AFC teams are preparing to play this weekend, the Denver Broncos are on the bye; it's an advantage, right?

Maybe not.

Consider this: The last time both No. 1 seeds advanced to the Super Bowl was 2009. Although, Peyton Manning was the quarterback of one of those teams—the Indianapolis Colts—they lost to the Drew Brees-led New Orleans Saints. And over the last five years, six of 10 No. 1 seeds lost in the Divisional round.

In fact, 2009 was the only time a Manning-led team won after having the Wild Card round off; the Colts lost in 1999, 2005 and 2007 in the Divisional round, and all Broncos fans remember their team losing last year.

Manning's playoff record is 9-11 overall and a shocking 1-4 after earning a first round bye week.

What's the deal?

Sports are all about finding a rhythm, building chemistry and staying at "game speed" from week to week. Routines are common and needed; breaking them can result in a breakdown at even the strongest points or positions.

Take 2012 for instance; the Broncos won 11 straight games heading into the playoffs and took the No. 1 seed, but instead of beating the Baltimore Ravens handily—as some thought they would in the week leading up to the game—uncharacteristic mistakes defined the Denver loss.

Everyone remembers Rahim Moore's silly play on the Hail Mary, but don't forget about Manning's two interceptions. After watching Trindon Holliday take the Broncos first possession—a punt—to the house, Manning stood on the frigid sidelines for extra time. His second pass of the day was an interception returned for a touchdown to give the Ravens a 14-7 lead in the first quarter. The second was even more damning, a throw back across his body to a covered Brandon Stokley, setting Baltimore up with the game-winning field goal in double overtime.

In 2007, he sat the second half of his Week 17 game and lost to the San Diego Chargers in the Divisional round, throwing two picks along the way.

2005 was similar, as Manning played only one series before sitting the rest of the game in Week 17, losing to the Pittsburgh Steelers in the second round of the playoffs while performing only so-so (22-38, 290 yards, 1 touchdown).

Go all the way back in 1999 to see the trend continue. Manning played most— but not all—of Indy's Week 17 game, but after the bye week, led his team to a Divisional round playoff loss to the Tennessee Titans. Even in only his second season, the 45.2 completion percentage seems crazy-low for the ever-accurate Manning.

Practices are one thing, playing in actual games—against teams doing everything in their power to not get sent home—is another. While Manning and his teams were allowed to rest and heal for a week, other teams stayed with their routines and kept playing football. Advantage, those without a bye.

Something encouraging for Broncos fans, though, is a buck in the trend. In 2009, Manning sat the second half of the Colts' Week 17 loss to the Bills, then had the first round bye, only to go on and win the next two games and advance to the Super Bowl.

So, what will we see this time around?

Will the bye week be a boon to the Broncos' chances, giving so many wounded players a chance to rest, or will it spell doom for Denver?

After their 2012 demise, John Elway said of the team, "You make your money in the regular season. But you make your legacy in the postseason as a player." Manning couldn't cash in that year. Would he this time around?

Also released the week of Black Monday was a poll reported on by

Public Policy Polling in which the Denver Broncos were named America's most popular team. According to the company, 14 percent of those polled sited the Broncos as their favorite team, in front of the Dallas Cowboys' 12 percent. In summarizing the data, it was pointed out that, not surprisingly, "One thing driving the Broncos' move to the top is the popularity of Peyton Manning."

As the week went on, Manning was named AFC Offensive Player of the Month of December, extending his NFL record of eight such awards; it was his fourth since joining the Broncos.

To end the week, the NFL announced their All-Pro teams, with four Denver players being represented. Right guard Louis Vasquez, wide receiver Demaryius Thomas, kicker Matt Prater and—of course— quarterback Peyton Manning, were all voted as the top players at their respective positions. The honor was extra special for Manning, who was the only one to be unanimously voted an All-Pro by the 50 media members who decide the team.

"It's a humbling deal," Vasquez, the fifth-year pro and first-year Bronco, said. "I have a great support cast with the rest of the O-Line, our offense and just our team in general. Just having great players around me helps. Everybody else looks that good; guys like Peyton just make you want to elevate your game. Again, it's humbling and I can't thank my teammates enough."

Manning's intangibles once again surfaced. Peyton the perfectionist demands the best out of his teammates, which is the only way these Broncos became the greatest offense in the 94-year history of the NFL. He led them to greatness, forced them to gel by taking over as a calming influence both in the huddle and locker room. Basically, Manning is like a player/coach; teammates don't want to disappoint him by doing the wrong thing—running the wrong route, lining up incorrectly or committing a penalty—because he's not afraid to give them an ear-full when they screw up. It's important to note not every quarterback can get away with this type of overbearing leadership, but Manning does because he earned the respect of teammates before joining them and certainly secured their trust over the course of two spectacular seasons commanding them.

There's no discounting the tremendously talented team John Elway and his executives put together, but without Manning's tangibles on the field and intangibles off it, the Broncos would most likely have been a shadow of this record-setting squad.

While Elway was the front office "yin," Manning was the on-field "yang." Together, something beautiful was created.

The day after their season finale, Broncos head coach John Fox talked about his team's potential playoff opponents. "Two of the three (San Diego and Indianapolis) have beaten us this season, we know that much," he explained to the media. "They all present problems. As I mentioned earlier, when you get in the playoffs they all present problems. That's typically why you have playoffs. So we'll just wait and see. We'll do some work on all of the potential opponents. We know it's going to be one of the three, we just don't know which one. We'll prepare this week as such."

It wasn't just that the three teams to beat the Broncos in the regular season were all alive in the playoffs, but that two AFC West rivals—the San Diego Chargers and Kansas City Chiefs—had postseason berths as well.

The interconnectedness of this season increased as it went forward through time; over the course of the season it seemed Denver was the team of destiny.

But before the Broncos could compete, they had to wait and see which opponent they would face. Luckily for them—as well as football fans across the country—the action on the gridiron was second to none that weekend.

In the AFC, the No. 6 seed Chargers flew to Cincinnati to play the No. 3 Bengals, while the No. 5 Chiefs were in Indianapolis against the No. 4 Colts. Because of their No. 1 seeding, the Broncos would play the lowest remaining seed, meaning it could have been the Colts, Chiefs or Chargers; the three hated "Cs". Over the years, both the "Bolts" and "Chefs" became rivals to Denver due to playing each other every season on a home-and-home basis, and the Colts—when they had Manning—could be counted on to beat up on the Broncos when they met. Playoff thrashings of 41-10 and 49-24 at the hands of Manning a decade earlier were still depressing for Denver die-hards.

No matter the opponent, storylines ran deep.

The first AFC contest of the weekend was a wild one. The Chiefs jumped out to a 31-10 lead at halftime in Indy, and were ahead by as much as 28 points early in the second half before Andrew Luck led the Colts on the comeback of the young century. Luck was as lucky as an Irishman, throwing three second-half touchdowns—including an electrifying 64-yard bomb to T.Y. Hilton for the game-winner—and even recovered a fumbled snap to dive the ball in over the goal line. It went down as Luck's first playoff win, 45-44 over Kansas City, who relied on defensive intensity all season long. That defense which was so stellar earlier in the regular season, was deflated by Indy.

San Diego vs. Cincinnati followed; it was another matchup of a top-tier offense versus one of the best defenses of the season. Usually an afterthought in the loaded AFC North, the Bengals won their division for the first time since 1990 thanks to the many playmakers in that dynamic defense, as well as the electrifying play of young receiver A.J. Green. In this game, however, they resembled the same old bumbling "Bungles," unable to score due to three second-half turnovers by Andy Dalton and unable to stop the Chargers' running game. The 27-10 loss went down as Marvin Lewis' sixth straight playoff loss as Bengals' head coach and Mike McCoy's first win as a head coach.

The upshot was that San Diego would travel to the Mile High City in a rematch of Weeks 8 and 15; each team had won their road contest during the regular season, with the Chargers' win coming on a short week for Denver.

In the NFC, the New Orleans Saints came back to beat the Philadelphia Eagles 26-24 on a last-second field goal by kicker Shayne Graham. It was the first ever road playoff victory by the Saints. They would play the No. 1 seed Seattle Seahawks the next week.

Finally, in a classic contest that resembled those phenomenal playoffs of yesteryear, the San Francisco 49ers and Green Bay Packers went head-to-head in four degree weather. Aaron Rodgers returned the week before to somehow get his Pack into the postseason by beating the Chicago Bears, and he was a major reason this was a back-and-forth battle. In the second half, though, Colin Kaepernick of the Niners came alive, rushing wildly and throwing for a 28-yard touchdown to tight end Vernon Davis in the back of the end zone for the fourth quarter lead. Later, his 11-yard run on 3rd and 8 set San Francisco up in field goal range and running back Frank Gore got them closer before Phil Dawson booted home the game-winning 33-yarder. The 49ers were off to North Carolina to face the Panthers the next week.

After those games, the Broncos (13/5) and Seahawks (12/5) remained the favorites in each conference according to Las Vegas, even though it had been five years since two No. 1 seeds met each other in the Super Bowl.

Denver had yet to play a postseason game; the team and Fox still had to prove they were beyond the bugaboo of the 2012 "Fail Mary." They'd get their chance against the Chargers exactly one year later.

Coming off the bye, getting rest and their two domineering wins to end the regular season—Denver had to feel confident going into their Divisional playoff game.

The offense scored on all five of its drives in the first half that Manning competed in when they blew out the Raiders, while the defense enjoyed back-to-back strong performances against the Texans and in Oakland. Momentum built for Denver's defense as the playoffs began and the offense was unquestioned as best in the NFL.

Of course, all that success is splendid, especially when considering how badly each and every team wanted to beat the Broncos. Denver fought through the best games each opponent could throw at them, learning from both victory and defeat.

Head Coach John Fox commented on the adversity throughout the season, "Again, all of those experiences hopefully are beneficial moving forward. Only time will tell. Each year your team takes on a completely different personality. This group is not the same group that was here a year ago. Obviously there is some carry over. Just like at the conclusion of this season, our team will not look the same next year. It's just the nature of our business. Again, we've got a great opportunity and what we do with it is why you do this."

That adversity began way back in January of 2013, a year before this time, and Fox was still using it as motivation to win in the 2014 playoffs.

"I think I have," Fox said regarding using the "Fail Mary" game as motivation. "There were a lot of guys that were on the team a year ago, whether it was the opening game of the season, or obviously we won't run into them again in this year's playoffs, but I think any time, any experience you reference, whether it's by me or maybe a teammate or one of the assistant coaches."

As you recall from Chapter 2 in this book, Fox admitted to not being able to sleep after conservatively ending regulation of the "Fail Mary" game by kneeling with 31 seconds left on the clock, two timeouts and Peyton Manning at quarterback, all at home. After taking the team to the playoffs in 2011 and 2012, losing quickly both times, Fox didn't want to be remembered as the coach that could get his team into the postseason but then lose right away. In fact, some in the media wrote that week that Fox was coaching for his job, and he may just have been.

Three straight AFC West titles are wonderful and all, but then, going one-and-done year after year isn't the goal.

As the attention turned from the previous year's playoff devastation to the coming week's matchup, Champ Bailey spoke with some veteran leadership.

"We know going into this game this team can beat us. They aren't going to sneak up on us," he told the media that week.

There was much surrounding the franchise in the week leading up to the game. So much happened, every day there seemed to be news involving either current or former Broncos players.

Knowshon Moreno was featured by *Sports Illustrated*, with a painting of him crying that now-famous river of tears from earlier in the year. The fantastic feature, written by Tim Leyden, focuses on Moreno's rags-to-riches-to-failure-to-success story, which is likely a reason behind the tears. Moreno, who grew up mostly with his grandmother after bouncing around many hole-in-the-wall apartments and homeless shelters with his separated mother and father, said he thanks God before every game by praying and runs through his entire life in the moments leading up to a game during the National Anthem.

Even without knowing the details of his life as were brought to life by the *Sports Illustrated* article, just an examination of Moreno's career illustrates a roller coaster ride. He was the No. 12 overall pick in 2009 and played well from the start, with nearly 1,000 yards rushing as a rookie. That is right when things started falling apart. He injured a hamstring his sophomore season, missing three games and saw declines in both yards and touchdowns (779, 5 TD). 2011 was his worst season as a professional, starting with that hamstring injury and then being placed on the Injured Reserve in Week 11. He fought back, but Moreno started 2012 on the practice squad. It seemed he went from first round pick to arguably the biggest bust in Broncos draft history.

Mid-way through 2012, Moreno earned the opportunity to start again, taking over for the injured Willis McGahee and exhibiting the best running in his professional career to that point. He carried the team through the second half of that season before tearing his knee again in the regular season finale, missing the "Fail Mary" game. In 2013, he was the most complete back he'd ever been, one of a handful of tail backs that could run effectively, catch passes out of the backfield and block in the passing game. Moreno racked up career-highs in every stat category in 2013; he was the Broncos' workhorse and also their emotional leader, deserving of the attention and the feature. Moreno's spotlight was well-earned.

For Peyton Manning, the accolades just kept on coming.

Manning was named the Colorado Hall of Fame professional Athlete of the Year for the second straight time. Others who were awarded the honor twice include Alex English (Denver Nuggets, 1982, 1985), Joe Sakic (Colorado Avalanche, 1996, 2001) and teammate Champ Bailey (2005-06). Manning—along with fellow Athletes of the Year selections Mikaela Shiffrin (skier), Kapri Bibbs (Colorado State University running back) and Barbara Szabo (Western State College) and 2014 Colorado Hall of Fame inductees—Otis Armstrong (former Bronco), Forrest B. "Frosty" Cox, Andy Gambucci, Darian Hagan, Todd Helton and Dorothy Mauk—were all to be honored in mid-April in Denver.

After annual television ratings were released, it was announced on the Denver Broncos official website that the team played in 10 of the top 25 watched television programs of the year. People all across the Rocky Mountain region are in love with their Broncos, no doubt, but with all that national television coverage, the entire country fell in love with the tremendous team.

On Thursday of that week, the Professional Football Hall of Fame released their 15 finalists. The team got some good news and some bad news. On the positive side, John Lynch was named a finalist to be part of the 2014 class. But, it also meant three others—Karl Mecklenburg, Steve Atwater and Terrell Davis—would again be looked over. The four former Broncos were all part of the 25 semifinalist list, with only Lynch moving on to the final round. After voting again, the Hall's committee has to decide on a maximum of five former players to be enshrined, complete with bronze busts in Canton, Ohio. I was there for John Elway's induction in 2004 and the place was electric with boisterous and proud Broncos fans. Elway was the first player from Denver's franchise to be inducted, with Gary Zimmerman and Shannon Sharpe added in recent years, as well as Floyd Little as a "senior player." It's a shame there aren't more Broncos players in the Hall considering how impactful their place is in NFL history. The first professional franchise from the Rocky Mountain region, a team to make the Super Bowl seven times, winning twice; Denver deserves more players in the Hall of Fame. But that argument is left for another time and place.

In the lead-up to the San Diego game, it was clear what the Chargers wanted to do. Everyone—the talking heads, fans and even the players—knew what to expect. San Diego beat the Broncos by running the rock with Ryan Mathews in Week 15, controlling the clock and simultaneously limiting Philip Rivers' ability to turn the ball over. It was the same game plan that Mike McCoy stuck with to beat the Bengals in the Wild Card round; Rivers threw a mere 16 times while the Chargers' three-headed monster of Mathews (52 yards), Ronnie Brown (77, 1 TD) and Danny Woodhead (54, 1 TD) combined for 183 rushing yards and two scores.

"I think that is the way they're set up," John Fox said of the Chargers' running strategy. "When you run the ball, it does use more time on the clock. The clock doesn't stop as much. It's part of the way they play. It's a very effective way to play."

The Broncos were ready for San Diego's ground and pound attack and Denver was the more physical team all day long.

But before the game even kicked off, Peyton Manning set another NFL record. This was his 21st appearance in the playoffs, most ever for an NFL quarterback.

As the Broncos' playoff slogan stated, it was "*Time to Ride.*"

After two weeks of waiting anxiously, the day finally came. No one knew for sure which Broncos team to expect, the record-setting one, or the one that was made to look mediocre by a handful of playoff-bound teams.

The weather was perfect for the Mile High City in mid-January, with a kickoff temperature near 50 degrees. It was sunny with wind gusting from the northwest.

One year to the day after the Divisional round playoff loss to the

Baltimore Ravens, the Broncos got their chance at redemption in two ways.

First and foremost, they had an opportunity to hold home field, to win and move on to the AFC Championship game. Second, Denver could earn some revenge on their division rival in the Chargers, who were the last team to beat the orange and blue.

Rod Smith, a member of the last Super Bowl teams and the greatest receiver in the history of the Broncos franchise, was there to lead New Mile High in chants before the game. It was incredibly loud all day long thanks to the Denver die-hards, setting a new standard for New Mile High.

Denver came out determined and physically dominated from the first whistle, likely feeding off the energy of their home crowd and their own angst-filled adrenaline. The amount of focus the team seemed to have was amazing.

They gave the ball to Philip Rivers and the Chargers offense to start the game.

The Broncos defense, which had gained so much confidence to end the regular season, seemed to stay on that Rocky Mountain high as they imposed their will early and often. Two plays in, the Rocky Mountain thunder rattled Rivers, causing him to call the team's first timeout. Six plays later, Rivers dropped back, only to have Shaun Phillips grab his jersey with one hand and pull the 6'5" and 228 pound quarterback to the ground in a feat of strength. It set up a 3rd and 16, and after an incomplete pass by Rivers fell short, the Chargers punted.

The sure-handed Eric Decker was sent back to return punts in the first half and did so without a problem, having even more success after the break. Manning and the Broncos offense jumped into the no-huddle and he made it clear he wanted to involve as many players as possible early in the crucial contest. Manning connected with five different receivers while letting both backs run as they pushed to the San Diego 29. From there, Montee Ball took the rock up the middle for eight yards and just before the Broncos could snap it on the next play, the Chargers called their second timeout of the game. Two straight first down runs by Ball gave the Broncos a first-and-goal at the three. Manning magnificently threw it low to Demaryius Thomas at the goal line for the first score of the day.

Thomas was completely covered and the defender even hit him early. There was no call, as is customary in championship and even Super Bowl games, but he still pulled off a fabulous catch with the ball hanging mere inches over the turf and over the goal line. The score was 7-0 Denver.

On the very next drive, the Chargers got into 3rd and 7 before a delay of game caused Philip Rivers to freak out. The noise was deafening. He threw a trademark temper tantrum, which Robert Ayers hilariously mocked, setting up 3rd and 12. Rivers has long been loathed by Broncos fans for his cocky attitude, the way he talked trash to Denver players and partly because he was a great player on a rival squad; seeing him flail his arms and fail due to their noise was wonderful in multiple ways. Rivers threw incomplete and his Chargers had to punt it away.

The Broncos took over near midfield. Two plays after the start of the second quarter, a third down conversion turned into a fumble by Julius Thomas. Thomas ran a slant and juggled the ball before finally securing it as he fell to the turf. It was ripped out by Jahleel Addae before the tight end's back end hit the ground. It was such a bang-bang play and yet the officials called it correctly on the field as a fumble, which was confirmed by the replay. Most of the time, NFL referees are top-notch.

After the first turnover of the day, the Chargers took over at their own 44. A quick first down run by Ryan Mathews of 16 yards started the drive, and just like that, they were into Denver territory. On 3rd and 3 though, Malik Jackson pushed off his block and when Rivers stepped up into the pocket, Jackson sacked him. It meant a lengthy 53-yard field goal attempt by Nick Novak who was off balance and had his plant foot slip out from under him, sending the kick wide left and too short.

Broncomaniacs rejoiced.

After getting the ball back with wonderful field position, Moreno was called for offensive pass interference, moving Denver back into a 1st and

20. But, a short pass to Moreno turned into 12 yards, a change of cadence from Manning pulled a San Diego player offside and Moreno ran for 11 up the gut and into the Chargers territory. Then it was Ball's turn, who ran it three straight times out of the shotgun formation, plowing ahead on draws. Another neutral zone infraction set up a 2nd and 1 from the 16. Moreno pounded the ball up the middle and hit defenders at the end of two bone-jarring runs down to the Chargers three and then Manning connected with Wes Welker on a quick out for the 14-0 lead.

Manning was doing everything he wanted. The Broncos offense was playing with balance, keeping the Chargers guessing as to what would happen next. The Sheriff's cadence was in the defenders' heads.

With exactly 6:00 until half, San Diego started at their 20 and two short passes to running back Danny Woodhead netted a first. After two short plays and an incomplete pass, though, the Chargers had to punt it back to the Broncos with 3:19 to go.

That's when Eric Decker had the opportunity to be a hero, twice, but instead made multiple mistakes on the big stage.

On the punt, in what could have been the tipping point of the game, Decker took a dive instead of running to freedom. Even though Trindon Holliday was the normal return man, Decker should probably have seen a few more punts during the season as he proved later in the year. He caught the ball at the Denver 23 and dashed straight up the field for 12 yards, dipped right and through two would-be tacklers, then dodged another tackler and pulled his feet through the punter's hands; Decker was off to the races! No! He fell down, despite the entourage of teammates, tripping himself up and face-planting at the San Diego 32.

It was reminiscent of 2012, when the "turf monster" jumped up to bite him in the ankles and take Decker to the ground during a Monday night game against none other than the Chargers. On that play—much like the 2013 version—Decker was out in the open. At that point in the Monday night game, the Broncos trailed 10-0 and nothing seemed to be going their way. That night ended well, however, as fans will recall the 24-point comeback and win, which was the largest comeback in the history of the franchise and the turning point of the season, the first of 11 straight wins.

Back to 2013; Decker's punt return still set Denver up with fantastic field position, a mere 30 yards from the end zone. Manning went to DT for nine yards and Moreno ran for no gain, setting up a 3rd and 1 in which the Chargers were again drawn into the neutral zone. The third such penalty allowed Peyton to run the clock to the two minute warning. A run up the gut for nine yards by Moreno and then a four-yard run put Denver on the San Diego four with 1:18 'til half. Moreno up the middle for no gain prompted a timeout with 40 seconds on the clock. The way Denver executed last-second drives was masterful, enough to give football aficionados goose bumps. On the next play, Manning rolled to his left and wanted to go to Welker, who was covered. At the last second Decker came open in the back of the end zone but the throw went sailing over his head. On third down Manning hit Decker in the upper chest and the receiver allowed the ball to bounce off his shoulder pads and into Donald Butler's hands for the interception. Looking back, it was probably the hardest pass by Peyton all season long; he was actually, miraculously getting stronger as the season wore on due to a lingering recovery from the neck surgeries.

So, two turnovers by the Broncos and yet they led 14-0 at the half. It could have and should have been by more and the two-score lead left San Diego feeling confident they could come back. Still, at halftime, Denver dominated every statistical category and in the physicality department as well; to wit, the Chargers wide receivers had zero receptions at the break and the Broncos led 13-4 in first downs.

The Broncos got the ball back after half, starting at the 36. Things went smoothly as the Broncos jumped into their customary no-huddle attack, mixing short passes and runs to perfection. But as they neared the end zone a miscue led to Manning taking the team's first timeout of the half far earlier than desired. Julius Thomas wasn't lined up correctly and Manning jumped all over him. It was another mistake by the tight end in his first ever playoff game. After the timeout, Thomas jumped early, a false start, moving the team back and forcing 3rd and 11. Manning tried to air it out over the middle to Welker but the ball fell incomplete and Matt Prater just hooked the kick in and over the top of the right upright with the help of the wind from 45-yards out. The score stood at 17-0, Broncos.

On the ensuing drive, the Chargers followed the Broncos' lead and called their first timeout of the half early, and then also kicked, but theirs was a booming 62-yard punt and touchback. At this point, longtime CBS ace play-by-play man Jim Nantz stated, "(This is the) Loudest I've seen it here." The noise was indeed intense, causing Philip Rivers to call three timeouts early in the game; two in the first half and one with eight minutes to go in the third quarter. It was the uproarious blue-collar crowd of days past; it was a wonderful display of fanfare to give the Broncos a true, old-school home field advantage. This was Old Mile High Stadium loud and it was clearly affecting Rivers and the San Diego offense.

For the third straight drive, Denver and their historic offense had a chance to put the game away, to stomp on the throat of the Chargers. But, for a third straight time, they couldn't come through. A 19-yard pass to Decker was followed closely by another neutral zone infraction as Manning used voice inflection to perfection to draw them off. Ball ran for eight up the gut and then converted another first down two plays later. After the fifth offsides call on San Diego, Denver was up to their 31; anything less than a touchdown wouldn't be good enough. But the Broncos couldn't gain five yards for the first down and Prater lined up to kick the 47-yarder which hooked viciously. It was only Prater's second field goal miss of the entire season, and he wasn't even close; it was a bit worrisome at the time, especially with close games in the playoffs often coming down to clutch kicks and narrow margins.

San Diego knew they were still in it; despite being down 17 points at the end of three quarters, they played like a team wanting to win. In the first play of the final quarter, Rivers found former Bronco Eddie Royal running away from Quentin Jammer and into open space for a 30-yard gain to Denver's 27. Three plays later, Rivers' offense was in a 3rd and 4 from the 16; he dropped the ball splendidly in over Keenan Allen's shoulder for their first score of the day. It was 17-7, Denver, with 13 minutes to play.

From their 19, the Broncos earned a first down on a pass interference penalty. Now at the 45, Manning hit Welker for eight, was incomplete to Caldwell and then connected with Julius Thomas for 17 to move to the San Diego 30. It was the first of many crucial catches by the tight end during this fourth quarter. Out of the shotgun, Moreno carried around the left for 14 yards and then followed Louis Vasquez for seven. Now down to the three yard line, the team called the same play; Moreno pushed in behind the wall of blocking by Manny Ramirez, Vasquez and Orlando Franklin, which blew the Chargers off the ball and drove the D-line through the end zone. This was old-school, smash-mouth football and Denver was domineering. The scoreboard showed 24-7, Denver, 8:12 to play.

When the Chargers got the ball back, they were in desperation mode, ditching the run game; all the passing paid off. On 4th and 5, Rivers unleashed deep to Allen, who ran up the sideline, then at and around Jammer for a 49-yard gain. It was San Diego's biggest play of the day and two snaps later, it was Rivers to Allen again for his second touchdown of the day, again running past Jammer. Jammer, the 34-year old former Charger, was called on when Chris Harris Jr. severely injured a knee in the third period; Rivers exploited the weakness to near perfection. 24-14 Broncos, 5:43 to go.

The game came down to this, an onside kick by the Chargers which they recovered after Decker allowed the ball to bounce off his chest. Again. Three gigantic gaffes by Decker continued to give the Bolts energy and life and they capitalized. San Diego had all the momentum at this point, which was quelled only slightly when Phillips came up with his second sack of Rivers on their first down. The veteran quarterback bounced back, going to his new favorite target when he and Allen accounted for another 17 yards, moving into Denver territory at the 47. Two plays later, it was Rivers to Allen again, this time for 25 yards, to the 17 and into the red zone. That's where the Chargers drive stalled. Two incomplete passes led to the decision by Mike McCoy, in his second playoff game as a head coach, to kick the field goal and the 30-yarder was drilled by Nick Novak. Denver only led 24-17 with 3:53 to play.

After making smart calls on the onside kick and field goal, McCoy decided to have Novak boot a mid-range kickoff, over the head of the ten Broncos awaiting another onside. Against most kick returners, it's a decent tactical play; the ball has a tendency to bounce around and after ten yards on a kickoff, it's live. But Trindon Holliday is so fast that he was able to speed up and catch the ball at the 21.

McCoy gave the ball back to Manning, who now only had to run out the final 3:51 in what most teams call the "four-minute drill." Everyone knows a two-minute drill is when a team hurries to score before time runs out; a four-minute drill is the opposite, a slowed-down approach used to bleed the clock. It should have been an easy task for the greatest offense of all time, and in the clutch, they came through to put the Chargers away.

Not before more miscues, though; Zane Beadles false started and Moreno lost two yards on a run, setting up 3rd and 17 from their own 20. Feeling pressure, Manning stepped up into the pocket, floating the ball to "Orange Julius," who was open after running an out-and-up, spinning to catch the ball on the sideline and tapping his right toe in for the first down.

Following the game, Manning said of the play, "The 3rd and 15 [sic], certainly it was a no-brainer there what you had to do. It was really disappointing that we were even in that position. We had been so good on first and second down the entire game, and we had a penalty, had run for a negative loss, had an incompletion. Great play call by Adam. Really was a big-time play call. Got them in the right look and a good catch by Julius."

That first down was huge because it kept the drive alive and allowed the Broncos to eat up more of the clock. On 3rd and 6 just before the two minute warning, Manning hit Thomas on a comeback route for another key first down. "The second one was another good route by Julius,"

Manning said. "I thought you saw that all game, Adam putting different guys in different positions. Certainly two huge third-down conversions, which were the difference in the ball game."

After the two minute warning, Moreno ran the ball twice for the game-clinching first down and they lined up in the victory formation for Manning to kneel away the win.

In the end, young tight end "Orange" Julius Thomas resembled Broncos legend Shannon Sharpe in the way he came through in the clutch for Manning. Sharpe caught a crucial third down pass from none other than the Duke of Denver in the Broncos' Divisional round playoff game in Pittsburgh to ice the Steelers on a cold day in January of 1998. During the first three quarters of his first ever playoff game, Thomas looked nervous and ill-prepared to play. He had multiple drops, and when he did catch one, he tripped himself up before gaining the first down. But down the stretch, like Sharpe, the tight end was massive.

"Julius was huge all game," Manning explained of his tight end's importance. "He's been huge all season. I think there's been a lot of changes since last year. We are much more experienced. We've been through a lot and have been in different situations. Those were two huge plays. I really loved Adam's aggressive calls. Julius and I have spent a lot of time working on those particular routes—after practice, in-practice. To me, that is one of the most rewarding parts of football. When you put that work in off to the side or after practice and it pays off in a game, it really makes it feel like it was worth it. Those two plays specifically were certainly worth the hard work."

The recognition is apt for two reasons; it gives us a glimpse into how much hard work it took for Manning to get on the same page with a basketball player turned tight end in Thomas, who was playing an entire NFL season for the first time in his life. We also get to see a little bit of what makes Manning tick. His work ethic is well documented, and the payoff comes during successes in the playoffs, as well as other games.

Thomas had some kind words about Manning, too. "He just keeps fighting. He doesn't get negative, he never gives up and he continues to fight and I think that's our motto as a team all year. We've gone through a lot, we've had a lot of key players go down but we just continue to battle."

It was a win. A sloppy and stressful win, but a victory nonetheless. In the game, the Broncos committed six penalties for 50 yards. There were seven dropped passes by Broncos receivers, one of which to Decker that could have put the Broncos up 21-0; his trip and fall on the way to the end zone on the punt return could also have given the Broncos a 21-0 margin.

An overarching theme was that Denver asserted their physical dominance throughout the entire win. Moreno and Ball finished off runs by looking to initiate contact, as did the most difficult player to tackle, Demaryius Thomas, on multiple occasions. Up front, the Broncos offensive line went into beast mode against the Chargers front; Moreno's game-clinching TD in the fourth quarter was a microcosm of the effort. And in the passing game, the offensive line allowed zero sacks of Manning. On the defensive side, pressure in the form of Phillips, Ayers, Jeremy Mincey, Jackson, and others haunted Rivers all night, as they racked up four sacks.

Often times, when two talented teams meet head-to-head, the most physical unit will win. That was clearly Denver on this playoff Sunday.

There were big plays both made and given up by former Chargers turned Broncos. Phillips had the sack to start the game and one on San Diego's final drive as he was a consistent pass-rushing threat all afternoon long. Vasquez blocked brilliantly once again, including his noteworthy push which Moreno followed on his game-clinching touchdown run.

Unfortunately for Jammer, the plays were not positive like his former and current teammates. Jammer allowed the Chargers' first passing score on the night from Rivers to Allen, and then gave Allen a 49-yard reception in the fourth quarter as well as the 30-yarder to Royal which set up their second TD of the game.

Maybe the most special variable that day was the noise of the Bronco faithful. Rivers and his offense couldn't get into a rhythm the first three quarters due to the roar, which caused false starts and the delay of game that led to the Philip Rivers meltdown.

The Denver Broncos were able to move on to the AFC Championship game for the first time since January, 2006. After making the playoffs for three straight seasons, this was the deepest they had gone, despite missing their second and third-best players, All-Pros Ryan Clady and Von Miller.

"Well, it's really been more than that," Manning said to Sal Paolantonio of ESPN when asked of the adversity the Broncos faced over the course of the year. "It goes back to the offseason. We lose a great player and the whole fax situation, and Von's situation and the offseason. We have dealt with a lot of adversity, distractions. Who loses their coach in the middle of a season? It just doesn't happen. Different injuries; Ryan Clady. So, we talked about that last night. We reflected last night in the team meeting of what all we have been through. And the collective unit has persevered. It hasn't been one person that kept us together, the unit has kept it together. This was a team win. We talked about, the only way we can win in the postseason is if the collective unit can come together. Tonight was a great example of that."

Also the night of the game, tweets came out showing Manning on the cover of *ESPN the Magazine* with celebrity actor Will Farrell, who was promoting his new movie at the time. It was all Broncos, all the time in the world of sports, and rightfully so. Manning was the man of the year in American sports, his story was the one to watch, the one to follow; he was the one to root for, just as Elway was in 1997.

Now fans around the entire country, not just Denver, were anxiously holding their breath to see what would happen in the coming weeks.

For Manning...

With his second touchdown pass, his 57 passing TDs became the most in a single season including playoffs in NFL history. Dan Marino had 56 in 1984-85, Tom Brady tossed 55 in 2007-08.

The win made him 10-11 all-time in the playoffs, 2-4 following the first round bye and 1-2 against Philip Rivers and the Chargers.

It also meant he improved to 6-0 since 2008 in rematch games, ones in which he lost to an opponent and then beat them later in the season. In those contests, he threw 13 TDs compared to one INT with a 113.4 passer rating. Manning and the Broncos had a chance to make it 7-0 against the Patriots the next weekend.

Denver was on the top of their game both offensively and defensively. The much maligned defense had seemed to turn the corner and had held three straight opponents to 20 or less points scored, something they did only once in the 15 weeks prior. Although that defense lost yet another starter in Chris Harris Jr. with an ACL sprain, thing were coming together at the right time for the Denver Broncos.

CHAPTER 11

MILE HIGH MAGIC IN THE AFC CHAMPIONSHIP GAME

"The spirit, the will to win and the will to excel --- these are the things what will endure and these are the qualities that are so much more important than any of the events themselves."

~ Vince Lombardi

Following the win over the Chargers, Peyton Manning and the Broncos would be playing Tom Brady and the New England Patriots in the AFC Championship game. Manning's words reflected his focus. "Tom Brady has just been an outstanding quarterback for such a long time, but the game next week is the Broncos versus the Patriots. I know there will be some individual matchups that will get headlines, but it will be a battle between two good teams. Teams that have been through a lot, that have overcome a lot to get to this point, and that's where my focus will be— trying to help the Broncos get a win against the Patriots."

Of course, the media focused on Brady-Manning XV, the biggest and most intriguing quarterback rivalry in recent memory, possibly the most impactful in league history.

"We're looking forward to it," Shaun Phillips said of playing the Patriots. "Obviously we're the two best teams in the AFC because we're playing for the AFC Championship, so what more can you ask for? That's what you want as a football player. Tom Brady is my second favorite quarterback behind Peyton. I really like Tom. I think he's a great player and a great person but what better way to do it? You want the two best teams going head-to-head and that's what's going to happen."

It was a matchup of the modern ages, a reason why the NFL set up Brady-Manning XIV during the regular season as a Sunday Night Football game; people love watching the best go toe-to-toe withone another. Think Ali – Frazer, Wilt Chamberlain – Bill Russell or Arnold Palmer – Jack Nicklaus; it developed into one of the greatest individual rivalries in American sports. Even football being a team game didn't dwarf the rivalry, because Manning and Brady are the two most recognizable figures in football. Even people that don't follow football know who they are, know their smiling faces and the products they pitch; like John Elway in the generation before them, each are ambassadors of the game. The league must have loved that it was Brady-Manning once again, this time for the AFC Championship. Brady's Patriots beat Manning's Colts in 2004 and then Peyton and the Colts bested Tom's Patriots in the 2006 AFC Championship game, a comeback for the history books.

Beyond Brady and Manning, the Broncos and Patriots were two supremely talented teams, each making the AFC Championship despite losing so many of their most gifted playmakers.

"They have a great football team, and they beat us a couple weeks back and our main focus is to see what they do that helps them keep winning," the incredibly talented receiver Demaryius Thomas said of New England. "We're going to work on it this week and hopefully come Sunday, whenever we play, we get the W."

As they went to work, more national news and supremely juicy storylines saturated the media.

Of course, first and foremost was Manning versus Brady, and it was clear to see who was better in head-to-head matchups to this point. Brady held a 10-4 advantage against Manning-quarterbacked teams, including the Week 12 victory in Denver on SNF. Interestingly though, Brady was 4-6 against the Broncos overall and his last playoff loss came in the Mile High City in the Divisional round of the 2005-2006 season.

Even though Bill Belichick was the coach and Brady the quarterback, Brady decided he and the Patriots were the underdogs, saying on WEEI sports radio's Dennis and Callahan Show, "We've got a bunch of underdogs on our team and we'll be an underdog again, and we'll see how that shapes up at the end of the week," Brady said. "But I know we're as tough, as physical as we've ever been, and that's how we're going to need to go out and play this game."

At this point in the season, both teams were seriously hurting from an injury standpoint. The Patriots were without five players for the entire year, all of whom were placed on the Injured Reserve in the preseason. Others, like physically gifted tight end Rob Gronkowski, defensive lineman Tommy Kelly, offensive tackle Sebastian Vollmer, linebacker Jerod Mayo, and running back Shane Vereen were all on the IR at some point in the season. That particular week, wide receiver Kenbrell Thompkins was also injured and sat out. It's where their slogan, "Next Man Up" came from.

Of course, almost every football team uses that saying, including Denver this year. For the Broncos, it was 13 men on the Injured Reserve, with five starters missing most or all of the season. Two more starters— Kevin Vickerson and Chris Harris Jr.—were each out for the rematch, while both had played in the first meeting six weeks earlier. Vickerson actually dislocated his hip in the loss to the Patriots and Harris tore his ACL during the victory over San Diego in the Divisional round win. But, luckily for the Broncos, they did have Julius Thomas for the rematch. The highly talented tight end who opened up the offense with his athleticism and size, sat in late November.

Overall, both teams were so beat-up and injured, it's a wonder they made it to the AFC Championship Game at all. But, it's also a testament to the supreme collection of talent each team was made up of, the vaunted leadership each franchise possesses from owner on down to the ball boys.

The Broncos were the better team, yes, but no one really saw New England as the underdogs due to their propensity for performing well in the biggest of contests on the biggest of stages.

The next most prominent storyline was Wes Welker playing against his former team in the Patriots. It was a bitter divorce between New England and the wide receiver. It was the team Welker called home for six seasons, the one in which he cemented his legendary status at the slot position. After franchise tagging him in 2012, the Pats wanted to low-ball Welker with a two-year $10 million offer. He began looking for a new team, and found a home in Denver. The Mile High City had everything he could have desired; a Hall of Fame quarterback, two tall and talented outside receivers, a pass-happy offense, and a shot at winning the Super Bowl. Even a private meeting with Robert Kraft couldn't change Welker's mind—likely because Kraft didn't change the offer—and a longtime friendship with Brady made the divorce that much more difficult.

Unsurprisingly, Welker fit in immediately with the Broncos. In the offseason, as reported by *USA Today*, Welker bonded quickly with Decker and Thomas during a practice at Duke University with Manning. They had performed the same ritual the year before with Brandon Stokley in Welker's place. Welker quickly found that the respect he had earned in New England transferred to his new environment. So much so, the ten-year veteran was named a captain by his teammates.

In the lead up to playing the Patriots, Welker was placed on the cover of *Sports Illustrated*, with a headline that read, "SO WE MEET AGAIN."

To add to the layers of interconnectedness, Josh McDaniels met his old team, the Broncos, that week. For Denver, it was the fifth former head coach or coordinator they faced that year; Mike Shanahan, Mike McCoy, Dennis Allen, and Wade Phillips are the others. Gary Kubiak could have been included, but he was fired, giving way to Phillips, who was the head coach of Denver in 1993-94.

McDaniels was the head coach in 2009 and part of 2010, then was rehired by the Patriots and faced the Broncos in their 2011 blowout loss to

New England, 45-10 in the Divisional round. It seemed unfair at the time, that a man could head coach one team, be fired with three weeks to go, and then hired by another team in the same conference before the postseason. Wouldn't McDaniels have an advantage on Denver and their offense? Without a doubt, it must have burned McDaniels, too, that he was playing against Tim Tebow, the kid he reached for to draft in the first round of 2009. This time around, McDaniels didn't affect the game as much and his offense was a shadow of its former NFL record-holding self.

Manning was named Most Valuable Player by the Pro Football Writers of America, making it his fourth (a record) such honor. He was the second Broncos player to win the award, with Terrell Davis taking it home in 1998. We must make the distinction here that this is not the NFL MVP, but a different honor which is still impressive. (This is a different MVP award. It was his fourth, fifth NFL MVP award...)

That same day, during his first AFC Championship week press conference, Manning was asked what "Omaha" means. "I've had a lot of people ask what Omaha means. Well, Omaha, it's a run play. But it could be a pass play, or a play-action pass, depending on a couple of things: the wind, which way we're going, the quarter, and the jerseys that we're wearing," Manning explained, jokingly, getting uproarious laughs from the usually reserved media. "It really varies, really, from play-to-play. So there's your answer to that."

Manning yelling "Omaha" before nearly every snap, sometimes in repetition, became a sensation all its own. It swept the nation, certainly grasping the attention of Nebraskans and companies located in Omaha; a group of local businesses banded together to raise $800 every time the Broncos quarterback uttered the name of their city during the Championship game, in hopes it would increase exposure. It undoubtedly did just that, becoming bigger than football itself.

Manning is more than just a football player, bigger than football, bigger than the sport. He's an ambassador of the game. He's funny, he's charismatic, able to joke and actually come off as humorous. In another life, he would have been an actor, and something says he'd be good at that, too. Manning's personable, intelligent and proof-positive hard work pays off; he's the type of athlete that makes for a perfect role model for children and adults alike. Humility and leadership are displayed on a daily basis by Peyton; it clearly rubs off on teammates and helps to propel them to greatness. In this "look at me" culture of football, where the spotlight burns so bright and cameras are intently focused on his every move, Manning rarely celebrates. Instead, he's shown yelling at himself or a teammate, not toward opponents.

In fact, "Omaha, Omaha!" became such a phenomena, it spawned T-shirts seen on display at the Omaha airport as well as other T-shirts by Denver based companies. He was the voice welcoming people to Denver International Airport and was also referenced on the gates to "Omaha!" Manning's reach went so far, he inspired multiple shirts like Denver's 5280 Shirt Shop offering their "Hurry! Hurry!" shirt, or the "#cutthatmeat" tee, commemorating a silly commercial from years past. Multiple Colorado grocery stores even created amazing displays of cases of popular blue and orange sodas. One in particular created a larger than life No. 18 jersey and the word "OMAHA" along with a goal post. Yet another had a 30-foot wide Broncos logo and two vertical "OMAHA OMAHA" spelled out with a cardboard cutout of Manning standing there, football in hand, looking to throw a touchdown.

He's become the greatest quarterback anyone's ever seen throw a football, but he's also blossomed into a cultural icon.

On Thursday, Von Miller tweeted a picture of himself post ACL surgery, saying he felt good enough to play that week. The Broncos could have used him, too. Despite sitting out the first six weeks of the season, Miller played well against the Patriots in particular, racking up two sacks and a forced fumble of Tom Brady early in the game to help Denver get out to a 24-0 lead in Week 12.

And while Brady had to pass the ball to bring his Patriots back to win—the biggest halftime lead given up in Broncos history—these Patriots had turned into a run team. They simply had to rely on the run. Without Rob Gronkowski and Kenbrell Tompkins, two of their most athletic pass-catchers, Brady had precious few targets. In the three games leading up to the AFC Championship, LeGarrette Blount took over; the 240-pound running back was faster than he looked and certainly a bruiser, rushing for an NFL best eight touchdowns over that span. Just like the week before with the Chargers, the Broncos knew the Patriots were looking to run the ball and that they'd have to stop Blount in order to win.

That week, Rod Smith was named the honorary captain of the Broncos. Smith played in three AFC Championship games as a Denver receiver, catching passes from both John Elway and Jake Plummer in those classic contests, going 2-1 as a player. He's well-known as the greatest undrafted receiver in the history of the league.

Here's what the ever passionate Smith had to say about the upcoming game.

"I just feel so good for those guys to get back to this moment. Last year was hard. It was hard for me. Honestly, as a player and being in that situation, I left the stadium, my stomach hurt bad—like somebody just took about 15 running starts and just punched me in the gut. I remember texting, actually on Twitter, Demaryius, I said, 'Man, take about a week or two off and then get back to work.' That's the only way you can get over it. You've got to get yourself back there. Some of the guys weren't here, so the good thing is they don't feel that pain, but the ones who did, I can promise you they're out there right now dialed-in, laser-focused, so the new guys will come and say, 'Oh, I've got to be on my game because I don't want to feel what they felt.'"

He was asked to predict the outcome. Smith said, "The Broncos win. Honestly, it's their time. It's time for this organization to get back on top, and you have to get through this challenge. This is probably one of the toughest challenges in the last ten years, honestly. I believe they have the personnel in this building—not just on the field—but in this building, they have the right personnel to go and get it done. I expect it to be big."

On Friday, Demaryius Thomas tweaked his knee in practice. It was a big-time scare for the Broncos as he was their No. 1 and most physical receiver. But, as Phil Simms told the story during the game, John Fox rubbed some dirt on the "owie" and said, "Yeah, you're okay."

Also on Friday, David Bruton was busting at the seams with excitement over playing in the game.

"It's not another home game. That's what it comes down to," Bruton said. "It's the AFC Championship Game. It's the last game before to you go to that 'ship. It's a dream game in two weeks. There is added pressure to this game. Everyone wants to go out and perform well, perform to the best of their abilities."

"I'm ecstatic. It's a one-in-a-lifetime deal," special teams captain Bruton explained. "Some guys get a chance to actually get to this game. We've been to the playoffs the past three years and I've never gotten to this game. So I'm extremely excited, happy and blessed for this opportunity."

In reality, none of the men who were on the 2012 team and went through that "Fail Mary" finish needed a pep talk. However, when Welker decided to talk, it may have hit home for some of the younger players and new additions.

Head Coach John Fox approached the veteran Welker, who was gearing up to participate in his fourth AFC Championship game, and asked him to talk to the team. That experience, coupled with his ties to New England, certainly. Before the game kicked off, Welker displayed leadership, giving a stirring speech to teammates about their opportunity that next day.

"I spent all day Saturday just putting something together," Welker said. "Watch a little film and different things like that of how I think the game needed to be played. The guys just went out and executed—and that's what it comes down to."

"He basically told us that it's hard to get to this position," the much younger receiver Eric Decker said. "And you've got to give it everything you've got because it's either win or go home. New England took it to us

Week 12. To get another opportunity, to be at home, we had to sustain that momentum that we had. He told us to come out, play strong and stick together through the good and the bad. And I think that's what we did."

"I even told [the team] this last week—I went to the Super Bowl in '07 and I thought I'd be back the next year, the next year after that and everything else. It's hard," Welker continued. "And you've got to seize the opportunity and take advantage of it."

With that, his Broncos were ready to beat the pants off his former team, the Pats.

This was it.

Brady had historically come through in nearly every one of his big games while Manning was questioned as the big game failure, despite his one Super Bowl ring.

This contest, their third AFC Championship facing one another, would go a long way in deciding the legacy of both men. And on this supremely sunny Denver day, Manning got the better of Brady.

Interestingly, each team was different than in their Week 12 meeting; the Broncos were without both Chris Harris Jr. and Von Miller—who sacked Brady twice to open the first game—but they did have playmaking tight end Julius Thomas back in action. For the Patriots, they were without Gronkowski, who enjoyed a touchdown in Week 12, but had found a shooting star in LeGarrette Blount who really turned it on for New England down the stretch run of the season.

After the opening kickoff, Denver's defense forced Brady's offense into a three-and-out when Dominique Rodgers-Cromartie deflected a third down pass.

On their own third down, Manning uncharacteristically bobbled the snap but somehow found a way to complete for a first to Julius Thomas. Then he hit Eric Decker on a crossing route for another first. Manning's men couldn't capitalize, punting the ball right back. A second straight three-and-out by the Patriots—this time, a deep ball batted away by Tony Carter—set the Broncos up with an opportunity they wouldn't waste.

In fact, it set up six straight scoring drives for Denver.

The first went like this; Manning to Julius Thomas on a crossing route, screen to Knowshon Moreno for 18 down the left sideline, incomplete pass then a rush for no gain both to Montee Ball. It set up a 3rd and 10. Manning hit Demaryius Thomas in stride on a skinny post up the middle of the field for the first down to the Patriots' 29. A play-action pass turned into a laser from Manning to Decker resulting in a first-and-goal at the 10. Manning threw the back-shoulder fade to JT, there was contact with Devin McCourty, the Pats' corner, but no call, despite John Fox's displeasure on the sideline. Moreno went up the gut for one, making it 3rd and 9 from the nine. Manning was rushed, a New England defender grabbed and turned him and forced the throw high over Decker's head. In came Matt Prater for the 27-yard field goal which he squeaked inside the left upright, 3-0 Denver.

When Brady got the ball back, at the 20, his first pass was a bullet to running back Shane Vereen. DRC went for the interception and missed, allowing Vereen to turn up field for a 24-yard gain. The next play, Brady went play-action deep to receiver Julian Edelman, who found his way past safety Mike Adams, but Brady uncharacteristically overthrew his pass-catcher. On 3rd and 5, Edelman ran a deep comeback, caught the ball for 18 and a first. No gain on a run and an incomplete pass, which was way wide of his receiver. This set up a 3rd and 10. Next, offensive pass interference made it 3rd and 20. A short pass and signature ankle tackle by Champ Bailey forced a third punt by the Patriots to begin the second quarter.

Broncos ball at their seven, the start of the longest drive of their historic season. Moreno took off behind a big-time Zane Beadles block for 11 yards and a first and followed with a one-yarder up the middle.

Then came a crucial play; Welker made a huge impact on the game, literally and figuratively. Welker and Demaryius Thomas ran crossing routes and Welker looked to "pick" or "rub" cornerback Aqib Talib; the harder than intended collision, which wasn't penalized, caused Talib to miss the rest of the game with a knee injury. Without the corner covering him, Manning went to DT over and over again, realizing and then exploiting the Patriots' weakness.

On the next play, 3rd and 9, Manning floated the ball over one defender and in front of another to Welker for the 14-yard first down. A short pass to JT and then a run up the gut with backup tight-end Virgil Green set up a third-and-short, a defensive holding resulted in a first down at the Denver 47.

The run by Virgil Green up the gut may have been a subtle jab at McDaniels, who had tight end Aaron Hernandez run multiple times with great success in the 2011 Divisional round win. Was Adam Gase watching that game? It's unknown, but the run was successful and gave Broncomaniacs a bit of satisfaction.

Two short incompletions meant a 3rd and 10. Moreno came to life. He got the handoff out of the shotgun, went between Vazquez and Orlando Franklin and hurdled a Patriot safety in a highlight-worthy play. He tripped during the process on what should have been a touchdown run. Still, he moved the team to the 11 and Ball rolled through three defenders during a run to the two. On third-and-inches from just outside the one, Ball collided into linebacker Dont'a Hightower for the first down. Then the Broncos utilized an old favorite from the 90s; they ran a play-action with Manning rolling out to his right, three receivers were open and Jacob Tamme caught the touchdown. Denver was dominating early with a 10-0 score halfway through the second quarter.

That's when Brady and the Patriots' offense came to life. On their first play of the following drive, he went into a seven-step drop and found a wide open Aaron Dobson for 27 yards up the middle of the field. Then Blount ran for three yards to the right, to midfield, and a screen to Vereen turned into a 13-yard gain. Two plays later, Brady rifled a 15-yard strike to the Broncos' 20, which was where the drive would stall. Terrance Knighton stoned the 240-pound Blount at the line, Danny Trevathan hit Edelman to allow only a two-yard gain and then Brady was forced to call a timeout.

On 3rd and 8, Robert Ayers pretended to go outside, darted inside and sacked Brady for an 11-yard loss, setting up a 47-yard field goal by Stephen Gostkowski, 10-3 Denver, 2:54 until half.

A first down hold meant the Broncos started their final drive of the half from just inside their own 10. A strike from Manning to Demaryius Thomas on an out-and-slant went for a quick 26. On the next play, it was almost the same exact route, just that Thomas was lined up more inside, catching the ball between the hash marks and being tackled at New England's 37. Then, Andre Caldwell's comeback on the sideline resulted in a third straight first down, to the 26. A quick out to Ball went for three and a two-yard out to Welker meant the Broncos called their first timeout of the half with 40 seconds to play. This was another example of Manning moving the team into scoring position during a four-minute drill. While it's rarely said, no one orchestrates the four-minute drill as well as Manning.

On 3rd and 5 from the 21, though, Manning found Moreno out of the backfield and a nice tackle saved the first down. While Manning visibly displayed wanting to go for it on fourth, Fox called the timeout and then called his quarterback to the sideline, opting for the field goal. Prater trotted onto the field and nailed the 35-yarder for the 13-3 lead just before the break.

With the score only at 13-3, this stat sums up the dominance by Denver's offense in the first half: First downs, 20-5 in favor of the Broncos. The Patriots wanted to run the ball, and yet, Blount was a non-factor in the first half, taking New England completely out of their game plan to start the second half.

When the Broncos took over and scored on a methodical march down field after the break, it further helped scrap that game plan. On 2nd and long from their 21, Manning found Decker on an 18-yard out. Now at the Patriots' 40, Ball took the handoff, danced and then pushed for five yards up the gut. A little bubble screen to Decker went for eight and another first down when Bubba Caldwell came up with a big block. Moreno then carried for three and Demaryius Thomas caught another short crossing route for four to the New England 20. The Patriots defense confused Manning a bit, causing him to call a timeout after the audible call wasn't made in time. After the timeout, though, Manning went to one of his favorite third down targets in "Orange Julius" for a five on a comeback route to move the chains. Inside the 10, Ball converted a crucial 3rd and 3 with a tough run. On the next play, Thomas shook his coverage and caught the touchdown on another slant. Their 7:08 drive was the longest of the season in terms of time, just seven seconds longer than the one in the first half, and pushed the Bronco lead to 20-3 with 7:52 to play.

No huddle was needed for the entirety of the drive. Manning was marvelous in putting on a show for the entire world of football to watch. Going back to the end of the first quarter and his rollout pass to Tamme, Manning threw 12 straight completions and went 13-14 after the touchdown to Thomas put Denver up 17. Simply sensational for a man many said couldn't perform at his peak during the big games. His passes were thrown with precision and Peyton was near-perfect during that stretch.

Brady battled with his Patriots, but he simply couldn't live up to the phenomenal display Manning put on. Still, Brady took a page out of Peyton's book and threw a multitude of short passes to a litany of receivers. He hit Dobson, Vereen and Austin Collie in succession for a first down. Stevan Ridley went for five behind left guard, and on third down, Brady found Collie on a deep out for another first just into Denver territory. The next play, Brady went for broke; a fake end-around turned into a deep pass to Dobson that Brady overthrew. And it was a good thing, too, because Champ Bailey was all over the receiver. It must be noted here that Brady was off all day long, missing open targets he regularly connected with. Vereen went for nine, though, and on third-and-short, Brady dove up the middle to move the chains again.

Now at the Broncos' 36, Ridley went around the right side for eight yards before Duke Ihenacho pushed him out of bounds. When Ridley ran again, Terrance Knighton completely blew up his blocker, hit the running back for a loss of one. On 3rd and 3, Brady was incomplete to Vereen when he was hit hard by Trevathan. The Patriots then decided to go for it on 4th and 3 from the 29 instead of attempting a 46-yard field goal. But Fox called a timeout before Bill Belichick could. Still, it was a complete Belichick move to go for it on fourth-and-short in a huge game; a high-risk, high-reward play-call by one of the gutsiest and greatest coaches in NFL history.

After the big timeout, Knighton sliced through Pro Bowler Logan Mankins to sack Brady and end the Patriots' drive with no points. It was the biggest defensive play of the game for Denver by the most massive man on the team.

Interestingly, as it was explained by Knighton, that timeout allowed him to get back onto the field. He was a bit gassed during New England's long drive, asking to come out after his 330-pound frame took the thin oxygen from his lungs. During that timeout, he decided, as a leader of the defense, he needed to be out there and then came up with the biggest defensive play Denver made all day.

"At first, I wasn't going to be in (the lineup) after that timeout," Knighton recalled to the *Denver Post*, after the postgame celebration in the locker room. "But then I thought, 'I have to be in there'. It was going to be a moment, and I was ready for the moment."

"I've been watching film on (Mankins)," Knighton said. "The last game when we played them I felt that I could have done the same move on him. The protection lined up right. It was the same thing I'd been seeing on film. I knew exactly what I was going to get. I knew what type of block he'd give me. I had to make the play. I did what I was supposed to do."

"All week in preparing, our defense just wanted to rise to the occasion in this game," Knighton said. "We knew our offense was going to get in a rhythm, and we just wanted to do our part."

They surely did just that, and now it was up to the offense, again.

With wonderful field position at their own 39, the Broncos started with a screen pass to Ball. It was sniffed out very well by New England for a loss of two yards. On 2nd and 12, Julius Thomas ran a quick out and then ran up-field for a gain of 12 to move the chains and move into New England territory. Then Demaryius Thomas went up the left sideline on a go route for a 30-yard gain. Ball then cut it back and gained eight yards; the Denver faithful cheered loudly as they knew they were a mere 15 minutes from going back to the Super Bowl for a seventh time.

To start the fourth quarter, Ball ran outside for a first, but it was called back due to a Julius Thomas hold. 2nd and 12 from the 22 and Manning went to the same Thomas who caught a short one, juked right as the defender slipped and fell to the ground, then gained the first down. A hold by Beadles meant backing up again, this time to the 18. Manning found Welker on a quick out, though, who lowered his shoulder into contact down at the two yard-line. A shovel pass to JT went for no gain followed by an incompletion (also to Thomas). Manning dropped the ball in perfectly but Thomas the TE couldn't hang on. So the Broncos had Prater kick the 19-yard field goal, 23-3 Denver with 12:05 to go. The same kicker who set the NFL record with a 64-yard boot against the Tennessee Titans earlier in the year made the shortest possible field goal, here.

Brady and Co. knew they had to come back and in a hurry, so he threw three straight completions. 18 yards to Hoomanawanui, 20 yards to Collie on a deep in, then 16 yards to Edelman on a comeback between the hashes—three first downs. Now at Denver's 26, he was incomplete to Edelman and then went to Vereen short for seven just as he was hit hard. An incompletion on another short pass to Vereen set up a 4th and 3 from the 19. This time, Brady connected with the Vereen for 12 on a quick out. After overthrowing an open Edelman in the end zone (again), Brady then found him at the goal line standing all alone for the team's first touchdown of the day. It was a 23-10 Denver lead with 9:26 to go.

Just like the week before, the Patriots kicked it short when the Broncos anticipated the onside. Again, Trindon Holliday accelerated to catch the ball at the 20. Manning's first pass was early to Demaryius Thomas. The second was thrown with perfect timing; Manning led Julius Thomas very well, allowing the athletic tight end run for 37 yards down the left sideline. Manning then audibled, Moreno ran up the middle for one and then to the left for one—injuring his ribs—setting up 3rd and 8. On that third down, the veteran QB tried to find Demaryius Thomas down that same sideline but was incomplete. Prater banged the ball through from 54 yards out and Denver led 26-10 with exactly seven minutes to play.

Knowing they'd have to score three times, Brady dropped back to pass. Over and over again. He was pressured and Vereen dropped the throw as Trevathan hit him. Edelman gained eight in the middle of the zone and then gained the first down on an eight-yard out. On second down, Vereen rushed for 11 and then Collie found open space for an 18-yard completion to the Denver 12, where Bailey tripped him up. Brady went to Edelman again and DRC blew him up at the five. With most of the defense in pass coverage, Brady took off up the middle for the touchdown run. The Broncos came through when Vereen's rush up the middle on the two-point conversion was stuffed by Phillips, Knighton and Trevathan.

Brady thrashed the "prevent" defense of Denver, but preventing the two-point conversion meant Denver still had a 10 point lead with 3:07 left on the clock. On that key play, Phillips circled around the tackle and hit Vereen in the backfield. After the play, Brady looked as if the game was lost as he hung his head in disappointment.

The onside kick flew straight at Eric Decker, who had lost the onside kick to the Chargers, but caught this one without a problem to basically secure the win.

From their own 49, Ball rushed for three and New England called their first timeout. Then, Tamme leaked out of the backfield into the open, catching a pass from Peyton before going 23 yards, making sure to stay in bounds. Timeout, New England, 2:48 to play. After the play, CBS showed Champ Bailey on the sideline, hands in the air, knowing he'd finally be going to the Super Bowl. The crowd chanted, "Su-per Bowl, Su-per Bowl..."

Ball carried up the gut for five, timeout, New England, their last. 2:41 to go. Ball carried again, this time for three, running the clock to the two minute warning. Ball carried, no gain, then outside to seal the win. One victory formation later and the Broncos were going to the Super Bowl!

It was Mile High Magic, a magnificent game by Manning and one of the biggest contests in Denver football history.

Shannon Sharpe, former Denver Broncos' great and Hall of Famer, was now a CBS analyst. Following the win, Sharpe said, "That's a special feeling. The fans in Denver hadn't experienced this on their home-field since 1998. There was a lot of pressure. There was a chip [on their shoulder] after losing the opening round of the playoffs. For them to get back here and have the season they have, to finish it off with an opportunity to win the Super Bowl, it's a special feeling."

On the podium, there were more proud Broncos.

Rod Smith, the game's honorary captain, presented the Lamar Hunt Trophy to Owner Pat Bowlen by yelling, "On behalf of the NFL, the AFC Champion Denver Broncos!"

"It's been a terrific group," John Elway said of the team. "They worked their tail off the whole year. I'm thrilled for them. They've been—the coaching staff, players, most of all, also, the greatest fans in America, right here."

"It's a great tribute to these players, this staff," John Fox said. "I couldn't be more proud of a group of men ever in my life. This goes to them (raised the trophy)."

"Bill's a great coach, a Hall of Fame coach, a great organization," Fox said graciously of the Patriots and Belichick. "This was a great game with two great organizations. We ended up on top and they had a great season."

"Well....surely very rewarding," Manning explained of the victory. "When you put in a lot of hard work into an offseason, into a regular season and it pays dividends with a huge win, winning the AFC Championship today. Like John said, we couldn't have done it without these fans. This team has been through a lot. We've overcome a lot of obstacles this year. It's been really gratifying to be part of this team. We have just kept our nose to the grindstone, kept persevering and it feels good to get this win today."

"I've always been an AFC guy," Manning explained of what it meant to have the Lamar Hunt Trophy in his hands. "I was glad to stay in the AFC when I came here to Denver. I'm biased towards this conference. What a heck of a day for football today. Unbelievable weather, playing a great team, great coach, great quarterback, great players and it feels great to get this win today."

It really was just that. A magical game on a magnificent stage; Denver only seemed more like the team of destiny with the win.

John Fox became the sixth head coach to take two different teams to the Super Bowl, the Carolina Panthers in 2004 and now the Denver Broncos ten years later. Those other five coaches are Don Shula (Baltimore Colts, Miami Dolphins), Dick Vermeil (Philadelphia Eagles, St. Louis Rams), Dan Reeves (Denver Broncos, Atlanta Falcons), Bill Parcells (NY Giants, New England Patriots) and Mike Holmgren (Green Bay Packers, Seattle Seahawks). Similarly, Manning became the first starting quarterback to lead two different teams to the Super Bowl, in the Indianapolis Colts and now the Broncos.

51.3 million people watched the game, making it the third-most watched AFC Championship game ever.

How many would be watching during the Super Bowl?

The NFL is all about unpredictability. It's the unknowing which makes us yearn for more. How can we grasp what is happening and how can we predict what will happen?

If we could, we'd be all be rich.

While the AFC Championship Game featured two of the greatest quarterbacks to ever lace up cleats in Manning and Brady, the NFC championship contenders were headed by two youthful, running quarterbacks and devastating defenses.

The San Francisco 49ers and Seattle Seahawks were the two most brutal, physical and demanding defenses in the league in 2013, with Seattle's being just a bit better with a few more marquee players with the ability to take over a game at any time.

Want evidence? The Seahawks forced three fourth quarter turnovers to beat the 49ers in the Championship Game. Up to that point, the 49ers were winning the game, leading 17-13 through three quarters. Then Seattle stole the ball and stole the show; a forced fumble set up a touchdown, a Kam Chancellor pick turned into a field goal and Malcolm Smith intercepted a Colin Kaepernick pass in the end zone to seal the deal. Seahawks 23 - 49ers 17.

It was only the second time in 20 seasons the two top seeds made it to the Super Bowl; did a classic matchup await fans?

CHAPTER 12

DEFENSE WINS CHAMPIONSHIPS

"If winning isn't everything, why do they keep score?"

~ Vince Lombardi

Immediately following Championship weekend, Seattle's Richard Sherman was the talk of the NFL due to his endorphin-fueled rant to Erin Andrews following Seattle's win in the NFC Championship Game. "I'm the best cornerback in the game..." His being an intense, young black man turned some off, and the narrative became, "Is Richard Sherman a 'thug'?"

During the "bye" week before the Super Bowl, snow fell on New Jersey—the first cold-weather city to host a Super Bowl in many years—which created two more narratives: first, that the Super Bowl shouldn't be played in the cold, and second, that Peyton Manning can't perform at his highest level in the frigid temperatures.

On Thursday, as it continued to snow in New Jersey, there was also snow in Denver. The Broncos took advantage and practiced outside in the cold, after plowing their Dove Valley practice fields.

The bye week before the Super Bowl is always a weird time in the NFL.

It's the first week without football in six months, yet everyone is awaiting the most important and possibly best game of the year.

And for the third straight week, a Broncos player was featured on the cover of *Sports Illustrated*. It was Moreno, then Welker and this week, Peyton Manning on the regional cover of the magazine. Sherman graced the cover of the Super Bowl XLVIII edition magazine for those on the west coast.

As the Super Bowl drew near, the already intense Denver die-hards became even more afflicted with what can only be called "Broncos fever." The City and County building was completely lit up with blue and orange, the capitol building flew two flags with Broncos logos and even the Pepsi Center—home to the Denver Nuggets and Colorado Avalanche—flew a banner that read, "We bleed orange, too!" Coors Field—home of the Colorado Rockies—also showed support with their "Time to Ride" banner at the home plate gate. Governor John Hickenlooper, former mayor of Denver, was clearly aware of how in love his Centennial State is with their Broncos. He temporarily renamed Colorado's 14ers—mountains which are 14,000 feet or taller—for Bronco players.

It wasn't just in Denver, either; Times Square had a billboard paid for by Texas Tech celebrating their three Broncos in the Super Bowl—Wes Welker, Louis Vasquez and Manny Ramirez. On Wednesday night, due to a victory by Denver fans on Twitter using hashtag #whosgonnawin, the Empire State Building was lit up in orange and blue, too.

Talk of Manning possibly retiring started during the lead up to the Super Bowl. When he was first asked, the aging quarterback said he'd love to continue to play. The next day, he said he honestly didn't know, and it seemed he may even lean that way.

Why retire? Manning had done everything as a quarterback. He had already won a Super Bowl, another would be icing on the cake. He set all the special single-season records earlier in the year. And during the Colts game, he got a standing ovation from the away crowd due to formerly playing there. In Houston, he again received a standing ovation after the

51st touchdown pass to Julius Thomas. How often do NFL games get stopped for standing ovations of one player? It's a rarity. Similarly, it was already like players were treating it as Manning's farewell tour, making it a point to talk to and shake the hand of the legendary QB, even if he did just thrash their team on the way to a win.

Maybe winning one more Super Bowl and going out on top—just like John Elway did in storybook fashion—would be enough to make Manning walk away from the game. The truth of the matter was, nobody knew for sure. But we all had a feeling if Denver were to win then Manning would ride off into the sunset just as Elway did.

Even Elway was playing all of his cards, hedging his bets, saying before the Super Bowl that, even with a win, critics wouldn't call Manning the greatest of all-time. Elway may have been right, but it also seemed like he was getting into the mind of Manning, trying to keep the most important and most valuable player on his roster.

Elway may have been calling the shots behind the scenes and trying to stay out of the way for the most part, but he also knew when to step forward to be the voice of reason. During all the media hoopla, John Fox talked about how Elway reacted following the Broncos loss to Seattle in the preseason.

"What's curious about this game to me is that both teams had high expectations, both outside and inside of their buildings," Fox said of the not-so-meaningless, preseason contest. "Sure that's easy if it happens all the time, but to be here, to be sitting here, it's a lot of hard work to meet those expectations. We had high ones going in. I think it was a preseason game. We did not play very well. Not taking anything away from them. It actually was a butt-kicking. When you get into camp you might have little lulls or whatnot. John [Elway] asked to speak to the team. He ended up doing pretty good. Hopefully, he pissed them off a little bit. I think it shook them up. Woke them up. I thought it had a good effect on us. We came back a little grittier and a little more determined. Camp can get kind of camp-ish. It got us going. I think it was good, but we still had two weeks of training camp to go."

"[It] was just one of those things where you think something needs to be said at that time," said Elway, to reporters during Super Bowl week. "We want this team to have a mindset that we want to be world champions."

"What I said was if you want to win a world championship, you don't go anywhere and lose 40-10," Elway explained. "To me, it seemed like some people thought it was okay, so I made sure to say it wasn't okay. At least I didn't think it was okay."

"It was basically, 'That's not our football team,'" wide receiver Demaryius Thomas said, "and he made it clear we have to do better, even if it was preseason."

"Just given his reputation, he demands a lot," All-Pro guard Louis Vasquez said. "That's all you really need."

That's leadership. Fox possesses a different, calmer style of leadership; it was Elway who seemed to light a fire.

As the teams got ready to play, Jimmy Johnson was the only one on FOX's broadcast to pick Denver, and he said of Manning, "If he wins this thing, he'll be in the conversation as the best all-time."

This wasn't just the biggest game in Manning's football career, it was also the biggest game for the Broncos franchise in 15 years. That's how long it was between Elway's retirement following his back-to-back Super Bowl victories, complete with the Super Bowl XXXIII MVP trophy, and this game. For one of the top football franchises, one that prides itself on winning, a decade and a half was too long to wait. This game had to be won.

Unfortunately, the Broncos never had a chance. They were bullied by the Super Seahawks from the get-go.

All the hard work of scouting, drafting and signing players through free agency, all the work in practice and throughout the pre, regular and postseasons; it all came down to this game.

In one corner sat the Seattle Seahawks, 2013's best defense in every single category and statistically the fourth-best defense of all time. They were known as physical from the front seven to their backfield, which was the heart and soul of the defense, nicknamed the "Legion of Boom." They brought the boom in both trash talking—Richard Sherman's rant following the NFC Championship game was classic, while his teammates chimed as well—and quite literally, on the field. They're ball-hawks—an admirable moniker given to men who fly to the football—making huge hits and causing turnovers.

In the other corner were Manning and his Mile High Scoring Machine. The Broncos put up video-game-like numbers on nearly every team they'd played all season long; even if scores had diminished a bit in the playoffs to 24 and 26 points, respectively, they had the firepower to blow the doors off any defense. It seemed that Manning and his men were too much for even the vaunted Seattle secondary. To wit, the NFL record concerning five men scoring ten or more touchdowns seemed like proof enough that Denver was too dynamic for anyone to stop.

That Bronco offense didn't show up. They never laced up their cleats that day; they weren't in the building as spectators. The Seattle defense was there. Bronco fans were there. The national media was in attendance. But the Denver offense? They stayed in Denver.

It went downhill following the coin toss. Joe Namath, resplendent in his white and brown fur coat, accompanied by a far-younger, beautiful woman, all reminiscent of his playing days in New York, tossed the coin before anyone chose heads or tails. Referee Terry McAulay caught the coin mid-air, had a quick laugh before the Seahawks called tails and Namath re-tossed; Seattle won and deferred until the second half, a strategy most teams have utilized in recent years.

Back in the Shanahan glory days—the last time the Broncos won the Super Bowl—he would hope to win the toss and then take the ball out on the field, score on a methodical drive and say, "We are the better team. Now play catch up." It was different now. Teams figured no matter what happened in the first half, if they got the ball to start the second, they could hopefully make something positive out of the possession.

So, Seattle booted it deep, eight yards into the end zone. Trindon Holliday, who hadn't been a story the entire season and no factor at all as the year wound down, decided he would take the ball out of the end zone; dumb move. He was tackled furiously by a swarm of Seahawks at the 14; it was the first of many violent hits.

As Denver approached the line, it seemed like just another game; the well-traveled Seahawks fan base roared and Manning decided to change the play. The veteran gun-slinger started towards center Manny Ramirez and before he—or anyone else—knew what was happening, Manning watched the football float over his head and bounce into the end zone where Knowshon Moreno somehow jumped on it to secure the safety for Seattle.

Two plays in and the score was 2-0 Seahawks.

The snap that came early shocked everyone. Fans, coaches…even players. You could see it in Manning's body language as he walked off the field with his head hung low, stunned. Despite all the preparation—not just this season but throughout their entire *lifetimes*—Super Bowl XLVIII was over before it even had a chance to begin.

In the days following the game, NBC Sports' "Turning Point" added audio to what happened on the field.

"I couldn't hear anything," Manning said to Zane Beadles on the sideline, "I called the cadence." That he did, as the replays, matched with his microphone, proved.

"I was thinking of telling you that," Manning second-guessed to offensive coordinator Adam Gase. "Start off silent when they're all hyped up."

Instead, it was the biggest blunder of the Broncos season, the quickest score in Super Bowl history and a harsh swing of momentum to start the game.

Denver had to free kick it from the 20, setting Seattle up with wonderful field position at the 37. On their opening drive, the Seahawks showed off Percy Harvin, who had become eligible to play for the first time all season that week, as he took a run around the left end for 30 yards with speed. Three plays later, on 3rd and 9, Russell Wilson connected with Jermaine Kearse on a slant for 12 yards and a first down. But on the next third down, Wilson tried to run to move the chains, dove and Duke Ihenacho pushed him out, short. The Seahawks drove but the Broncos defense bent and didn't break, allowing only a 31-yard field goal by Steve Hauschka, 5-0 Seattle.

"We'll never regret the points," Pete Carroll said at the time of his decision to kick the field goal instead of going for it on fourth-and-inches.

Denver's defense, focused on stopping the conventional running of Marshawn Lynch, was doing just that during the onset of the contest. While the story was all about Seattle's physical attack, the Broncos' defense came out strong in the Super Bowl, as well.

Denver got the ball back and had to find a way to produce positive yards. Knowshon Moreno carried behind left tackle Chris Clark for three yards, was stood up and thrown down after the whistle. On second down, Manning found Demaryius Thomas on a short crossing route; Kam Chancellor lit him up with a huge hit.

Boom!

The most difficult player in the league to tackle was tossed to the ground, going backwards multiple yards following the vicious collision. The crowd "oohed." It was only a sign of things to come. That sore shoulder bothered the Broncos' most physical player the rest of the game, taking him out of his element a bit.

On 3rd and 5, the veteran quarterback progressed through his reads to find Julius Thomas underneath for three, but not enough for the first down. It was three-and-out for the best offense in the NFL's modern era in the most important contest of the season. Manning glared at the video board in New Jersey as he walked off the field, searching for something, *anything*, that would give him an edge, give him a detail into just *how* the Seahawks were so dominant early.

As Seattle linebacker Bobby Wagner, who tackled Thomas, stood there with his hand in the air in a fist to symbolize fourth down, the Broncos offense ran off the field past him, with their tails between their legs. Wagner, posing in that fearsome way, was a symbol of the Seahawks standing tall, lording over the Broncos that chilly February night.

Seattle got the ball back at their own 28 and utilized the short passing game to push into Denver territory. Wilson, who seemed to allow his nerves to get the best of him to begin his first Super Bowl, rolled out to his left and found Golden Tate on the sideline for eight to move the chains. Wilson then threw a laser to Doug Baldwin on a crossing route for a first. On a crucial 3rd and 5, the youthful Seattle quarterback cocked back and floated one deep to Baldwin down the left sideline for a 37-yard gain. Baldwin was able to gain separation from Champ Bailey on an out-and-up route which used another player as a pick; Bailey saved the touchdown at the six. A holding call on Max Unger pushed them back to the 16, though, where a two-yard run by Lynch and two incomplete passes by Wilson killed the drive. One of those incompletions went laterally to Harvin. John Fox challenged and the play was upheld—correctly—as incomplete, not a fumble as the Broncos hoped. That could have been a massive momentum swing back in Denver's direction; no dice. On the next play, Wilson had Kearse in the back of the end zone, but an amazing play was made by Nate Irving, knocking the floating football away and saving the touchdown. Hauschka had to kick and connected from 33 yards making it 8-0, Seahawks.

After all that, the Broncos were down only one, measly score. This was the team that put up an NFL record 76 touchdowns in the regular season, one TD seemed simple.

"Hey, we're the best damn offense to ever play this game," Wes Welker yelled at teammates via 'Turning Point'. "We gotta start doing it. Just go out there, play with your heart, do your assignment, we'll be just fine."

Not against this domineering defense.

On first down from the 20, Manning hit Welker for five yards before he was hit by Chancellor. Hey, it was a start. On the next play, Moreno ran into a wall of Seahawks defenders, having the ball ripped from his grip—like tigers ripping meat from bone—before he was down and Zane Beadles fell on it for a two yard loss. That play was an example of Seattle simply being more aggressive, having more fight than the Broncos that day. On 3rd and 7, Cliff Avril overwhelmed Orlando Franklin on the right side; feeling the pressure, Manning stepped up and threw both prematurely and high. Wagner jumped up at the line. The pass went soaring two feet out of the tall Julius Thomas' reach and into the awaiting arms of Chancellor.

First the unimaginable safety and now the unthinkable interception on only Manning's second pass of the game? The bad just kept getting worse. When the Broncos needed Manning to come through the most, he folded under the pressure literally and figuratively.

"I didn't have much time," Manning explained to Thomas, acknowledging he should have waited another second to throw the ball. Thomas agreed. The Seahawks' pass-rush was just too much, too powerful for the Broncos M*A*S*H* Unit on the offensive line.

Seattle started with the ball in Denver territory, at the 37, and began the drive with another Harvin end-around to the left for 15 yards. On the final play of the quarter, Wilson threw to tight end Luke Willson over the middle for five, down to the Broncos 17.

When FOX came back from the highly profitable timeout, they showed the stats from the first quarter. It was ugly for Broncos fans. Seattle had run 22 plays for 148 yards and possessed the ball for 11:41. Conversely, Denver's seven plays netted 11 yards with 3:19 in possession. This was a nightmarish scenario.

After the timeout, Marshawn Lynch pounded the rock up the middle for six yards and a first down at the 11. A second straight run by him resulted in a loss of one when Danny Trevathan knifed in and sat the bruising back down. To reiterate an earlier point, Trevathan and Denver's D came to play against Lynch that day, and their effort kept the team in the game as long as possible. Wilson found Doug Baldwin for a gain of seven, setting up a 3rd and 4 from the five.

On that critical play, Wilson ran right and finally threw it to Golden Tate in the back of the end zone. The pass wasn't going to be completed, but Tony Carter was called for pass interference because he wasn't looking for the ball. It was a bad call that set up the Seahawks on the one; two plays later, Lynch dove in for the 15-0 lead, 12 minutes until halftime.

"It's just, I don't even know how to explain it," Champ Bailey said to Tony Carter on the sideline after the score.

"They're just like controlling the game," Carter replied.

"This will help right here," Bailey explained. "If our offense can get something going."

This was it; Denver had to not only sustain a drive, they had to put some points on the board. And just when they need to most, the Broncos remembered how to play football.

They remembered, at least, for a few minutes.

As Vince Lomardi said, "It's not whether you get knocked down, it's whether you get up."

After Holliday was hit hard by Chancellor on the kickoff, the Broncos started at the 16 and Denver's short passing game started heating up. Manning went to Demaryius Thomas on two bubble screens in a row and Moreno carried behind Franklin for five and a first. 19 minutes into the game, the best offense anyone had seen since 1950 finally had a first down.

Another short pass went for seven, Moreno ran for two, and a first down catch and stretch by Thomas was followed by a deep ball to him, incomplete. Ball ran right for one and then Welker caught a pass and went up field for 16 to the Seattle 43. DT reeled in his fifth pass of the drive, this one for nine yards, and on third down Ball moved the chains behind Beadles' pull-block. But Beadles then tripped a Seahawks defender who would have hit Manning, putting the team in a 1st and 20. Manning threw a screen to Jacob Tamme for a two yard loss, but a check to a run by the quarterback and a strong carry by Moreno of nine yards got them in a more manageable 3rd and 13.

Then, the play of the game happened.

Manning stood tall after taking the shotgun snap, surveyed the field and saw Thomas had gotten past safety Earl Thomas deep. But as Manning cocked his arm to throw a bomb, the bull-rush of Clint Avril pushed Franklin into the quarterback and Avril hit his forearm with great force, causing the ball to float helplessly through the air.

In those few seconds that seemed to take many minutes, the Broncos' Super Bowl hopes and dreams vanished in thin air.

Malcolm Smith made a play on the ball while Moreno stood there—maybe shocked into disbelief by the unprecedented pounding his team was taking—and picked off the football, rumbling 69 yards for a touchdown and the 22-0 lead.

All year the Broncos had been through more adversity than anyone could have dreamed up; where was the unflappable Manning to step up and lead his team through it all? As the 12th Man that descended on New Jersey celebrated like the wild bunch they are, Manning trotted to the sideline and stared blankly, likely replaying what could have been in his mind. He then stood there with his helmet still on, mouth agape, shaking his head, rejecting what he was experiencing was the truth.

Was this real life? It seemed like a terrible nightmare to Broncos fans, and probably to Manning, too.

Why this was the turning point of the game became clearer after watching the film again. If Manning is allowed to throw that ball, it could have resulted in a touchdown. He wasn't checking down to Moreno, as it originally seemed, Manning was going deep to Thomas who had not only burned Sherman, but Earl Thomas too. In Week 16, DT blazed past Texans' defensive backs in a similar fashion and Manning put the ball right on the money; there's no reason to think this pass wouldn't have become a score, as well. It could have been 15-7 or even 15-8 if Denver decided to go for two. Instead, it was 22-0.

It was sad. It was like getting beat up by a bully in high school; going home and telling your big brother, only to have him get beat up by the same bully.

Seattle literally bullied the Broncos. They kicked the Broncos' butts, stood over them with foot on throat and asked, "Do you want some more?" When Denver kept playing, they kept finding the same kind of fight; at every turn, around every corner, there was a Seahawk to punch a Bronco in the mouth. Denver was dominated in the physicality department from the first whistle. It wasn't even close.

Seattle meant to set the tone and did just that. They played their physical, smash-mouth style of football; Denver's wimpy dink and dunk passing couldn't overcome that intimidation. The Broncos then quit, which was the most disheartening bit of it all.

If they didn't quit at the site of Smith intercepting their leader, Manning, and then rumbling the length of the field only to emphatically dunk the ball on the crossbar of the field goal post, they certainly quit just after halftime.

But the beating wouldn't stop for Bruno Mars and the Red Hot Chili Peppers yet; Seattle kicked off and Holliday was again walloped on the return. He fumbled and the Seahawks got the ball, but the play was reviewed and reversed; Holliday held on just long enough for his left knee to touch down before the ball came out.

Manning threw to Julius Thomas on first for five and on third down found Demaryius Thomas for 19 yards on a back-shoulder fade. He went to Welker for five, then JT settled into a soft spot in the zone, catching a pass for 11, which resulted in a first down at the Seattle 27 at the two minute warning. okay, surely they'd score now, right?

On first down, Manning was incomplete to "Orange Julius" when his route was impeded by Earl Thomas, no call. Moreno caught a screen and went up field for six yards on the next play. But then Louis Vasquez false started—3rd and 9—and Moreno caught another pass, this time for seven yards before Chancellor stopped him.

At the Seahawks 19, John Fox had a decision to make; would he conservatively kick the field goal and put points on the board or go for it on fourth-and-short? Fox went for it after asking Manning and the quarterback saying, "Let's go, we'll get it."

Manning's pass to Demaryius Thomas was tipped at the line, though, falling incomplete and resulting in a turnover on downs. In the days after the Super Bowl, rumors swirled like the wind at MetLife Stadium that Prater—who had been sick the week before—was still not himself, missing 40-yarders in pregame warm-ups. Prater's condition could have influenced Fox to not go for it. No matter how Prater was feeling though, down three scores, going for it was the right decision.

Yet again, the Seahawks' superior physicality, their ability to dominate in the trenches, was a big reason Manning didn't have the time nor the space to throw. While Denver's offensive line worked the Chargers and Patriots D-lines in the playoff games leading up to the Super Bowl, they were used and abused by Seattle's front seven. This time, it was Chris Clark being pushed back and into Manning's face by Chris Clemons, who batted the ball off course.

A close up of Manning's face was again shown, and again he seemed to not believe his own eyes, and was then more visibly frustrated than earlier in the game.

Two dives by Lynch took the teams to halftime. As they left to the locker rooms, Sherman yelled to his teammates, "We whooping they ass!" That they were.

The halftime show was so-so, tough to watch and enjoy if you were a Broncos fan, and a few days later Flea of the Chili Peppers admitted they weren't even playing live.

The same could be said of Denver's football team. They weren't playing live; they even weren't present. It was the first time all year the Broncos were shutout at halftime and only the third time in their 19 games they were even trailing at the break.

Still, the eternal optimist Denver die-hards out there were saying, "It's only a three-score game." Yes, the biggest deficit ever overcome in a Super Bowl was ten points, as the FOX halftime guys pointed out, but these were the record-setting Broncos.

So, a half an hour after they left the field, the teams ran back on the gridiron and Prater kicked it "deep" to Percy Harvin. Instead of the ball going out of the end zone, like it did 64.8 percent of the time during the season, Prater's boot only went to the 13, bounced straight into the air, and then Harvin took off. When the ball bounced up in the air, the Broncos players left their lanes and went after the dangerous return man, diving and missing. He dipped and danced and shook all the Broncos special teamers as he ran down field for the game-clinching touchdown. Denver planned to kick it that way, short, and Seattle adjusted on the fly to return the kick up the middle of the field for the touchdown. 12 seconds into the second half Seattle led 29 to zero.

The camera showed Manning watching the replay of the touchdown and disbelief turned into anger; exactly how the rest of Denver watched on that cold Sunday night.

Down four scores, the Broncos tried to mount a drive and once again couldn't. Quick, no-huddle passes to nearly all his receivers helped Manning march the offense down field. But Manning attacked deep with DT on Sherman, incomplete, and then went to Welker but Chancellor broke up the pass and swaggered around the field. On 3rd and 10, the Broncos ran a draw and then punted from Seattle's 39.

Conservative play-calling in the biggest game of the year? Ridiculous. Manning was visibly upset he was being called off the field, yelling in disgust; so were fans.

Seattle responded with one first down run by Lynch and a punt, Denver started at their own 45. John Elway looked on with a long face from one of the luxury boxes above the turf at MetLife Stadium. Just as he smugly smiled as his team dismantled the Texans, his body language was representative of the entire team that day.

Two positive plays resulted in a first down and it seemed like the team might finally gain some momentum. Then Manning hit Demaryius Thomas, who carried the ball like a loaf of bread during the 23-yard gain and was stripped with ease by Byron Maxwell. The injured shoulder likely had something to do with the fumble, and Thomas should be saluted for playing through the pain of that injury. Still, he could have carried the ball with both hands if he truly was hurting that badly. Another swing of momentum went the way of Seattle.

If the Broncos' offense were men playing against boys during every other game that season, in the Super Bowl, it was the Seahawks who were giants—performing more like mythical creatures than mere mortal men—and the Broncos were babies.

With 5:55 remaining in the third quarter, the game and NFL championship was definitely in the bag for Seattle. That point was further emphasized when Kearse caught a pass from Russell Wilson, turned towards the end zone and couldn't be taken down by four Denver defenders; this had turned laughably bad as Broncos bounced off of the wiry receiver. 36-0, Seahawks, 2:58 left in the third.

At that point, with all the pressure now gone, the vaunted Broncos offense came alive. Talk about too little, too late.

Manning went to Welker short, huge hit. Then to Julius Thomas short; he was smacked painfully in the knees by a helmet. And on third down, a pass interference call on Seattle's Maxwell as he was all over DT—the first penalty called on the Seahawks defense—moved Denver up to their 41. During the drive, the Denver defense was shown on the sidelines, looking distraught.

A 12-yarder to Welker and an 11-yarder to Jacob Tamme pushed the team to the Seattle 36, where Welker caught a crossing route for 22 yards and another first down. From there, Manning and DT connected for the team's first and only touchdown, followed quickly by Welker's two-point conversion, 36-8, Seattle, end of the third quarter. Thomas' touchdown snag was nothing short of spectacular; he had to reach high while being pulled down by Maxwell, still securing the ball for the score.

To start the fourth, Prater kicked it onside, it went too far and Zach Miller recovered at Denver's 48. The Seahawks made it clear they weren't going to quit trying to score. Wilson threw the ball five straight times, including a deep one up the seam to Kearse and a 10-yard touchdown to Baldwin, who ducked under three defenders. It was 43-8, Seattle, with 11:45 to play.

The Broncos started from their 13 and Avril batted down a pass. Then Denver advanced to the 28 on a pass interference call and Demaryius Thomas set a Super Bowl record with his thirteenth catch of the evening, up to the 45. But, that drive stalled and they turned it over on downs again when Manning's arm was hit by Michael Bennett on fourth.

With only 9:48 to go, Seattle looked to run out the clock, running six straight times before giving it back to Denver on downs. Four plays later, Manning fumbled the ball away when Clemons beat Clark around the edge again; nail in the coffin. And a steak through the heart of Broncos fans.

If Vince Lombardi were watching the game he would have yelled, "What the hell's goin' on out there?!" Instead, the Lombardi Trophy was shown being walked in by a man wearing white gloves, as it was about to be presented to the Seahawks for the first time in franchise history.

There were four turnovers by the Broncos and none for the Seahawks that day. It wasn't just Denver's mistakes. Seattle forced the turnovers, and turnover margin is the best predictor for victories in the NFL. The ballhawks led the league in the regular season with a plus-20 turnover differential; Denver was middle of the pack at even.

And it's not just about turnovers, it turns out, but explosive plays, as well. As former Baltimore Ravens head coach and NFL Network employee Brian Billick wrote in 2011, "Toxic Differential" is the most important indicator of wins in the National Football League. To find the Toxic Differential, first you must find the "Explosive Differential," which is the number of 20-plus yard plays gained versus 20-plus yard plays given up. Then, add that result with the turnover differential, and what you'll see over the course of a season is the cream rising to the top.

In 2013, the No. 1 team in Toxic Differential was, you guessed it,

Seattle. They were best in the league in turnover differential (+20) while their +46 in explosive differential gave them a +66. Only the Philadelphia Eagles had a better explosive differential (+48), and despite being the highest scoring offense of the modern era, Denver was fourth in explosive differential (+17). The Broncos were fifth overall in 2013 at +17, which means their turnover differential was zero. In the Super Bowl, the Toxic Differential seems to reflect the lopsided result.

The Seahawks enjoyed seven explosive plays and they gave up four, which is an explosive differential of +3. Add in their four turnovers, and their Toxic Differential is +7. On the opposite end, the Broncos' numbers are -4 and -8. Numbers don't lie.

The Seahawks went four-and-out to finish the game and dumped Gatorade on Head Coach Pete Carroll, twice. Denver ran three more half-hearted plays. The game was thankfully over.

It wasn't just that the Broncos were beaten. It was that they were beat-down so brutally. That was hard to accept. That Denver couldn't run their offense or string together multiple positive plays was disheartening, disturbing even; how the Seahawks won so thoroughly was extraordinary. Eerie were the similarities and parallels to the preseason game against the same Seahawks.

Following the game, Peyton Manning talked to the media about the loss.

"From the very get-go, a turnover on the first play of the game, giving them a safety, not the way you want to start a game," he explained. "For whatever reason, we couldn't get much going after that. But I give Seattle a lot of credit. They're an excellent football team and they caused a lot of our mistakes. At the same time, we just didn't play well tonight."

The understatement of the year from the understated Manning.

It's certainly plausible that the team was woefully underprepared; something completely out of the ordinary for a Manning-led squad. The Broncos, who prided themselves on being more prepared than any other team, were anything but that in this game. Two weeks should have been plenty of time for Manning and offensive coordinator Adam Gase to discover some weaknesses and fine-tune a game plan fit to give the Seahawks fits. But that's not what happened.

Instead, the Broncos were indefensibly conservative in a game they should have laid it all on the line. Down four scores, you punt from the Seattle 39 in the third quarter? Why? Handing the ball off in a "third down and a cloud of dust" situation? What good does that do?

All of that studying, all of the looking at printouts between drives along with Manning didn't prepare either Gase or his quarterback for this, the most important game of either of their lives. Gase was an up-and-coming coordinator, a supposedly superior offensive mind, but there was no creativity, scheming or exploiting of weaknesses this week. For Manning, this was a possible legacy-defining game, either way. A win would have likely cemented him as the greatest quarterback of all time, as Jimmy Johnson alluded to before kickoff, and the loss left him stuck with the "choker" label, the one that says he can't perform well enough in the most crucial of contests.

Those two weeks of game planning gave Seattle, not Denver, the upper hand. Both Richard Sherman and Seahawks defensive coordinator Dan Quinn stated as much following the win.

"All we did was play situational football," Sherman said during his victory party, as Robert Klemko of The MMQB reported. "We knew what route concepts they liked on different downs, so we jumped all the routes. Then we figured out the hand signals for a few of the route audibles in the first half."

According to Klemko, Sherman showed off some of those hand signals and further explained, "Me, Earl [Thomas], Kam [Chancellor]… we're not just three All-Pro players. We're three All-Pro minds. Now, if Peyton had thrown in some double moves, if he had gone out of character, we could've been exposed."

That says something. Football, much like the art of war, is all about surprise and deception. Catch your opponent off guard, you can beat him to the punch, or beat him to the edge for a big play. While Denver's dynamic offense was wonderful at doing this all season long, they were too bland, too easy to read when it mattered most. Instead of Manning having the upper hand and knowing what the defense wanted to do, it was the reverse; Seattle's secondary stars studied tape, learned their foe and used that information to dismantle Denver's offensive attack.

Defensively, while the performance was far from perfect, the unit kept their offensive brothers in the game through the first half. Harvin was a huge X-factor, but he didn't beat Denver. They fought tough, despite having little to no pass-rush all game long, and it was clear their focus was on stopping Lynch. The all-star running back gained only 39 yards and due to his blazing speed, Harvin gained more yards (45) on just two runs.

It also became clear how much the Broncos missed their own starters in the secondary. Chris Harris really grew into a strong nickel/cornerback and his speed, along with Rahim Moore's, left gaping holes for Wilson and his no-name receivers to exploit. Their missed tackles on that third quarter passing touchdown were completely inexcusable and were reminiscent of the Super Bowl loss to the San Francisco 49ers in 1989.

Special teams was a joke, just like it had been all season long. Denver wasn't exceptionally strong in that phase of the game when 100 percent healthy, but one way injuries devastated the team was by forcing practice squad guys and others not necessarily fit for duty to step up and perform on the biggest stage. Look at the Harvin kickoff return touchdown for instance; Jacob Tamme tripped himself—even though it looked like he was blocked slightly from behind—and linebacker Brandon Marshall flat missed the tackle. Even Prater, who had been the most consistent special teamer all year, was off. His kicks came up short and the offense was unable to rely on his big leg to save them from failed drives.

Coaching-wise, it wasn't even a contest. The Broncos were out-coached from the first whistle; Fox proved again he didn't know when to throw the challenge flag and he also proved that being conservative rules the day for him. In the Super Bowl, there's nothing to lose besides that game itself. There's no playing for next year. The team should have let it all hang out, gone for the gusto, gone for it on fourth down inside the opponent's 40 yard-line.

It was all too reminiscent of the loss to Baltimore the year before. When pitted with the big decisions, Fox always chooses the conservative approach. Conservative doesn't win championships. Ask Bill Belichick, he'll tell you himself; going for those high-risk, high-reward plays pays off more often than it seems prudent.

And, weirdly, Fox moved the team away from their hotel on the Saturday before the game, to one at the Newark Airport. Supposedly, his thinking was to get the team away from distractions—like their families and fans roaming around the hotel—and yet it back-fired big time.

In the days after the loss, some other information came to light. It's possible the Broncos didn't play well because some of them were out partying hard during the lead up to the Super Bowl. Ronnie Hillman was infamously pictured at a gentleman's club with a dancer—and rumored to be with teammates—while Von Miller was reportedly turned away from a Seahawks victory after-party. Is it possible the Broncos, who looked like they were treating it like a business trip when they traveled in suits to New Jersey, were actually playing too hard?

On what he told the team during their final meeting of the season, Fox explained, "That I was proud of them. Obviously we're all disappointed. Disappointed for everybody in this building, No. 1, disappointed for the fans. But, it was a great season. We accomplished a lot. This team went through a lot. To walk out with your heads high. I know there is disappointment—it will take a while to go away for all of us, but at the end of the day, it was a successful season. Fifteen-and-four is not real shabby."

Therein lies a possible problem with Fox's mentality. He's always calm and cool and positive and maybe finding the silver lining isn't always the best way to go. Maybe being satisfied with 15-4 isn't enough. To be Super Bowl champion, you can't be "not real shabby," you have to be willing to take nothing less than being the very best.

When the Broncos were beaten badly by Seattle in the preseason, Elway must have really had some choice words for the team after this Super Bowl blowout. Two days after the loss, he and Fox addressed the media, with this fiery response by Elway ending the press conference.

"And I'll say one thing: I kind of get the sense that these questions are about 'How the Hell are we going to overcome this?' Well, the bottom line is, 'Sure. It's not even 48 hours away from the game.' But I will tell you this: right now the focus is on what happened instead of how we got there and what we did this year, what we went through as a team. But I say that the farther you get away from this, the less you concentrate on just that one game, the more you recognize the whole season and really what we did as a football team and really as an organization. And I'll tell you what, I'm very proud of that.

"There are some changes we've got to make and we'll make those. But the thing is, we can use that as a game that, 'okay, we now know what it's like to be there, now we're going to use that as the experience of we've been there but we've got to start with step one again and start with the offseason program.' And April 21st—everybody that knows it comes in here and the people that we bring in here when it gets to 85-90 guys on the roster, John [Fox] readdresses this team the first time and again it's to get back and be World Champions. The goal has not changed and it will not change. We will use this as an experience that we went through, be disappointed that we didn't play better, but the bottom line is this organization and what [Owner & CEO] Pat Bowlen wants from this organization—that has not changed and it will not change. The bottom line is we're going to work as hard as we worked this year, if not harder, and continue to do that with the mindset that we want to be World Champions and we're going to do everything we can to get there."

During the presser, Elway admitted, "I'm not over them (blowouts of the 80s) yet. I just add this one to it (laughing)."

It was similarly tough for Broncos fans to take the abysmal loss. And beyond that, it made one wonder if—or for how long—it would have an effect on Manning as well as his teammates.

This is no excuse—there aren't any excuses to make for the Broncos in the blowout loss—but a few weaknesses were glaring due to injuries. The offensive line, which was missing three starters, couldn't protect Manning. Ryan Clady would have been a big boost to pass protection at left tackle, though Chris Clark played well all season. The errant snap that led to a safety and should have never happened. If Dan Koppen is in, maybe it doesn't start that way. On the defensive side, a lack of pass rush was evident; Von Miller, Derek Wolfe and Kevin Vickerson certainly would have helped that. And it's more than likely both Chris Harris and Rahim Moore could have helped in the secondary.

But, in Denver, the future remained bright. Making the Super Bowl is a positive in its own right and the Broncos would look to go back time and time again. With Elway at the reins of the Broncos, making the big game seemed like an inevitability instead of a hope.

As he said following the season, "We remain relentlessly committed to delivering a world championship to our fans." He wasn't just blowing hot air; the proof was in the pudding.

Ten days after the season ended, Elway was re-signed for three additional years and the title of "General Manager" was added to his Vice President of Football Operations tag. It was much deserved.

In 2010, the Broncos went an abysmal 4-12. It was their worst record, their worst season since the 1960s. It wasn't acceptable and a major reason why Josh McDaniels was fired. In the three years since Elway took over the big office in Dove Valley, the team went 34-14 in the regular season, won the AFC West three straight times with back-to-back 13-3 campaigns. In the playoffs, they were 3-3 over that same time, making it to the franchise's seventh Super Bowl. Yes, they were blown out, but considering all those injuries, it was a testament to the truly talented team Elway had built in Denver.

It wasn't just his personnel acumen that made Elway amazing at his job, either. He's a true leader of men, gaining and retaining the respect of his players, coaches and anyone within the organization, as well as media members he dealt with. Charismatic and competitive, Elway was able to use his personality to govern his environment. For Elway, there's only one way, to win.

Record Recap

Peyton Manning became the quarterback with the most losses in NFL postseason history when the Broncos were blown out by Seattle. With a victory, he could have improved to 12-11 all-time in the postseason, with a 2-1 Super Bowl record. Instead, his 12 losses were the most ever and he was on the wrong side of .500 in all postseason games as well as the biggest of games, Super Bowls.

Manning set a single-game Super Bowl record for most completions with 34, while Demaryius Thomas' 13 receptions were also a single-game Super Bowl record.

It was also the first time in NFL history a game ended 43-8 and 36 straight points was the most by one team in a Super Bowl. Denver was the first team to not pick up a single first down in the first quarter.

Seattle became the first team to score on a safety, kickoff return and a pick-six in Super Bowl history.

For the Denver Broncos, the franchise dropped to 0-3 all-time in Super Bowls where their players wore predominantly orange jerseys.

Overall, the Broncos dropped to 2-5 all-time in Super Bowls, with all five of their losses being blowouts. Seven Super Bowl appearances represents a tie for second-most, five Super Bowl losses is the most of any team, a dubious NFL record for Denver.

During the loss, sometime in the second half, my brother looked over and said, "I guess we know what Dad must've felt watching the Broncos in the 80s." And just like that, it had come full circle. See, we grew up in the glory days. Not that every year was winning Super Bowls and parades; I was too young to remember the 80s Super Bowl blowouts, but the Broncos were only so-so during the early 90s. That much I do remember. Then Mike Shanahan came along with his revolutionary offense and changed everything.

The Broncos really turned it on from 1996-1998; the loss to the Jacksonville Jaguars at home set up the team up for a redemptive storyline with back-to-back Super Bowl victories. In 2005, Denver was close, losing to the Pittsburgh Steelers at New Mile High in the AFC Championship Game. But they hadn't been back to the big game until 2014. 15 years.

In a way, it was something special for our generation of fans. We lived through all the fun and excitement of the late 90s Super Bowl wins, now we were experiencing the heartbreak that the older generations had felt four times over before Elway's helicopter, Terrell Davis' Mile High Salutes and Shannon Sharpe's HULK flexes.

That was what being a fan was all about, supporting your team after they break your heart because you know they're just as heartbroken.

As far as blowouts are concerned, the one in 1989—55-10 at the hands of Joe Montana, Jerry Rice and others—still stands as the biggest blowout in the history of the Super Bowl. So, at least there's that.

I've always believed that it is better to get to the Super Bowl and lose than to not get there at all. It makes sense on many levels; the Broncos were shown all over the national media in the weeks leading up to the big game, their logo was plastered all over Times Square and all around Colorful Colorado. For a few fun weeks, Colorado caught Broncos fever, just like they used to in the 60s, 70s, 80s and 90s; it was certainly a special time to be a fan, a time all of us will fondly remember for years and generations to come.

Why? Because the Broncos are taking us on the ride of a lifetime, setting the bar so high for offenses in this now offense-dominated league, playing at levels never seen before, and possibly, never to be seen again.

The ride isn't over. The Elway-Manning era rolls on and fans have more to look forward to. What can we expect in the coming years?

CHAPTER 13

A LOOK BEHIND AND A LOOK AHEAD

"Don't succumb to excuses. Go back to the job of making the corrections and forming the habits that will make your goal possible."
~ *Vince Lombardi*

For the Denver Broncos, 2013 was the best of times; it was the worst of times. The season brought with it very high highs and the lowest of lows.

The season started off with a bang, a seven-touchdown performance by Peyton Manning and a drubbing of the reigning Super Bowl champion Ravens. Revenge for the "Fail Mary" game? At least, a little bit. That kicked off six straight wins, most of which were blowouts, and three 50-burgers hung on opposing defenses. A 13-3 finish, multiple NFL and franchise single-season records and a third-straight AFC West championship; those were the highs.

They extended their season first with a playoff win over divisional rival San Diego and then against nemesis New England, overcoming the Belichick-Brady problem.

But the lows—the utter embarrassment that was Super Bowl XLVIII, the physical domination, the turnovers and uncharacteristically poor play—were certainly disappointing to organizational leaders like John Elway, down to the players and fans.

What hasn't been a disappointment? Manning's play overall, especially in the regular season.

His 92 touchdowns in two years with the Broncos is the most ever in NFL history per Broncos PR man Patrick Smyth. Think Elway is happy with Peyton's production?

When the Broncos landed Manning it was considered a gamble, which seems ludicrous to say now. To sign a 36-year old signal caller is silly, especially considering the five-year, $96 million contract Peyton and the Broncos agreed to. Signing a 36-year old fresh off of four neck surgeries was a major risk; some wise people believe the universe rewards those who take risks.

For Elway the executive—early in his new front office career—landing Peyton Manning was a major tipping point. It was a career-defining move, similar to winning his first Super Bowl was as a player.

One question initially was whether Elway possessed the business acumen and overall savvy needed to run a team. Many former players had tried and failed miserably—Matt Millen in Detroit is the favored example— few have succeeded. One success story, however, is that of Ozzie Newsome with the Baltimore Ravens. Mr. Newsome has constructed multiple Super Bowl winners in his time with that franchise.

Manning was magnificent in his first season with the team. Despite not being full strength, being in a new town and playing with new teammates, Manning and the Broncos offense achieved rapid and remarkable success. If Manning was indeed a "noodle arm" as one report said, if he had lost that playing prowess somewhere along the way between zero and four neck surgeries, he would have failed miserably and so would have Elway. He'd have been endlessly compared to Millen.

Instead, Manning's success and the team's success boosted both quarterbacks' legacies. After an additional year of physical training, creating a playbook with coaches and connecting with teammates, Manning realized his true potential and reestablished himself as the greatest quarterback in the NFL. He was unquestionably that in 2013.

Let your mind digest this for a moment: In 1997, the Denver Broncos enjoyed the No. 1 offense in the NFL as far as points-scored and points per game are concerned. It was Mike Shanahan's third season and he continued to prove he was to be on the cutting edge of offense in the NFL as the offensive production improved annually.

Never before had a team from Denver done as well as Shanny's Broncos; the zone-blocking scheme was so simple it worked to near-perfection, Terrell Davis followed through the holes so large you could drive a Mack truck through with room and Elway was still able to utilize his hobbled legs to run the bootleg off the play-action pass. Davis carried the offense; it was a different, more physical game, in those days.

TD was a power-back who had the grace of a ballet dancer. He was most comfortable running through traffic, bucking off defenders when the time was right. But, he didn't necessarily seek out contact; Davis would dip and dash one way or the other, only to juke would-be tacklers out of their cleats and run past them in seemingly simplistic fashion.

You're going to tackle Terrell Davis—the top running back in the world for a solid two-year span—head-on? You'd have better luck rolling a royal flush off the flop in the World Series of Poker's Main Event.

In fact, during the 1997-1998 seasons, basically the only way people tackled Terrell was from behind. He never possessed the speed to finish off 80-plus yard runs, but sub-80? Good day, good evening and goodnight; the TD train has just departed. Davis scored a whopping 15 rushing TDs in '97 to lead the league, and then was the best touchdown scorer again in '98 with 21. TD was a machine; a gentle, intelligent, happy, caring and incredibly gifted touchdown machine.

Behind John Elway, Terrell Davis is the greatest Denver Broncos player, ever. Though, due to his lack of longevity in the league, he will likely forever be held out of Canton's hallowed halls.

In 1997, the John Elway-led Broncos scored 472 points.

Let's fast forward to 2013 when Denver's offense scored a staggering 606 points. A staggering 128% of the points scored in '97.

Peyton Manning and his offense were grown men. Opponents were like mere babies. Opposing offenses were laughable. And for defenses, Manning and the Mile High Scoring Machine were like the Borg; the Broncos' playbook was simply more advanced than anyone had dealt with before. Resistance was futile.

Manning's men were the first and remain the only team to ever score so many points. The first number is a six. Six. Hundred. Points. That's 100 touchdowns without extra points, safeties or field-goals (their total was "only" 76 TDs).

The stark contrast between 1997 seems clear. It's not just that the 2013 Broncos scored a whopping 132 more points. The difference lies in the styles in which the teams played. While Shanahan's teams were all about gaining the tough yards—the crucial, game-changing and game-winning yards—on the ground. Peyton's Broncos were predicated on passing with precision to a multitude of deadly receiving threats. Of course, Manning would have liked to have a running back like Davis to pick up that crucial fourth-and-short in the Super Bowl instead of risking the conversion on a pass, which was tipped in the game.

The game of football has evolved significantly since 1997, and the NFL has developed into a passing league. But what Manning and the Broncos' offense have been able to accomplish has set the standard unfathomably high. In 2013, it was as though Manning and his men were playing on a shorter field than anyone else because they could score at any time, from anywhere.

All that offense is astounding, but with the surreal success brings two problems.

First and foremost, it's almost impossible for Broncos fans to not expect more in 2014. Rewind to 2012—Peyton's first in the Mile High City—and the offense was better than anything they'd seen in nearly a decade. It was the best all-around quarterback play Denver die-hards had ever experienced. Manning clicked immediately with teammates and commanded the strong leadership role throughout. 2013 was bigger and better in every single way. What will 2014 bring?!

This is a call to fans: Temper your expectations of 2014; at least on the offensive side of the ball. Yes, the team improved in every way offensively in 2013 compared to 2012, but to expect that to happen again, even on an incremental level, would be nothing more than fool's gold. Head to the hills to experience fool's gold; in Denver, a city founded on the shiny, valuable mineral, we want the real deal.

Secondly, what we all learned from 2013 is that even the most explosive offense is simply not enough, alone, to win the Super Bowl.

That's why Elway—who's quickly becoming known as the most aggressive executive in the league—went back to work, attacking free agency furiously.

But first, he was re-signed by the team. Following the Super Bowl blowout, Vice President of Football Operations John Elway took another step toward possibly becoming the next Broncos owner; his contract was extended three years and his title expanded to include General Manager. He also re-signed Jack Del Rio and recently extended John Fox's contract through 2016, which were major moves. With Del Rio, they created stability in a role that had been anything but consistent in Denver. The Broncos went through seven different defensive coordinators in seven seasons before Del Rio; he's been the man on that side of the ball since 2012. With Fox, the Broncos solidified their head coach for another three years. The major leadership pieces are no longer in any kind of flux.

Elway attacked free agency with the same aggressive fury that defined him on the football field. Hit Elway? He's going to hit you back. And then go for the jugular with a last-second score.

Following their Super Bowl XLVIII demolition and demise, Denver was called soft by some. Were they? It sure seemed so.

After coming out and playing more physically than the Chargers and

Patriots in those playoff victories, the Broncos were caught off guard, allowing the Seattle Seahawks to jump all over them with aggression. That physicality by Seattle never relented and Denver never fought back.

They needed warriors, gladiators, men that seek out contact, ball-hawks much like the "Legion of Boom."

The NFL is a copy-cat league and Elway's first acquisition was in direct emulation of the Super Seahawks.

T.J. Ward, star safety and formerly of the Cleveland Browns, is known as the "Gronk Killer" for injuring Rob Gronkowski of those rival Patriots. He's a welcomed addition, bringing the toughness that was lacking, especially in the secondary. Ward is extremely talented; he understands how to play the run and throws his body into bigger backs with a reckless abandon. He's a willing hitter and sure tackler who doesn't let go after getting his hands on a ball-carrier. Ward doesn't seem to ever give up on plays; he competes with great instinct and has very quick hands. All-around, he's a top-tier safety in his prime; a massive upgrade from the older Mike Adams.

Elway continued to rework his secondary. While Dominique Rodgers-Cromartie was solid in 2013, he wasn't great and certainly not physical enough. The Broncos tried to rework a deal with DRC, but when it fell through, Elway swooped in to steal a second truly talented player from the Patriots in Aqib Talib.

Talib is a legitimate No. 1 cornerback, with lockdown abilities. He proved that much in the AFC Championship Game before being injured as he rendered Demaryius Thomas virtually useless for an entire quarter. Talib's got great ball skills and wonderful body control, which allows him to adjust on the fly, putting himself in position to make plays on the ball as it flies through the air. He's averaged ten passes defended and three interceptions per season for a reason; he's a ball-hawk. Like Ward, he plays with great, natural football instincts; it's like the game comes naturally to him. Talib makes plays on the ball quickly, undercuts receivers with ease. He's also a willing tackler and understands the importance of wrapping up.

An intangible that will help Talib gel with the new unit? He and opposite starting cornerback Chris Harris Jr. played together at Kansas.

That's right, Chris Harris; after ten years with the Broncos, the team had to move on and cut cornerback great Champ Bailey. This opened the door for Harris to move from slot man to the No. 2 corner opposite of Talib.

A few weeks later in the 2014 Draft, Elway and Co. went and got cornerback Bradley Roby from Ohio State, a young man they hope will contribute right away. The theory is that, on passing downs, the big and fast Roby will come in as the No. 2 man and Harris will move over to the slot.

In the Super Bowl, Denver's starting defensive backfield was DRC and Bailey at corners, Adams and Duke Ihenacho at safeties and Tony Carter in the slot. In 2014 the projected starting DBs are Talib, Harris, Ward, Rahim Moore and Roby. Besides the rookie Roby, it's a definite improvement at every position.

They say imitation is the sincerest form of flattery; Seattle should be flabbergasted.

Adding Ware was extremely intelligent. The Denver defense was much better in 2012 than 2013, and a great deal of that can be attributed to the phenomenal pass rush generated by the dynamic duo of Von Miller and Elvis Dumervil. With Miller expected to play much more of the 2014 season than 2013—sans ludicrous legal and substance abuse troubles as well as the torn ACL—and Ware lining up opposite him, the Broncos should be able to bring that one-two punch needed for toppling tackles and opposing quarterbacks once again. Ware has racked up double-digit sack numbers in 7-9 professional seasons, going through a shoulder injury in 2013. He'll be hungry to prove himself with a new team, one capable of winning the Super Bowl.

More good news is that Derek Wolfe should return to health in 2014. This has led fans to create the moniker the "Von Ware-Wolfe" front. Just the sound of it sends shivers down quarterbacks' spines; seeing them play together should be a real treat.

Manning couldn't pass in Super Bowl XLVIII because his offensive line was overpowered by the Seahawks; Elway imitated them by adding to his arsenal of pass-rushers while simultaneously bolstering the secondary. Passing will be difficult against Denver's defense in 2014.

There was a reaction to that poor, inconsistent O-line play by the Broncos' front office, too. Zane Beadles left in free agency, Orlando Franklin was moved from right tackle inside to left guard and Chris Clark was moved from left tackle to right tackle with Ryan Clady coming back from injury. Depth was added there, as well, with the addition of free agent center/guard Will Montgomery and two draft-picks, Michael Schofield and Matt Paradis.

The final piece of the puzzle, perhaps, was to be seen on the offensive side of the ball. When the Broncos lost No. 2 receiver Eric Decker to the New York Jets, Elway signed Emmanuel Sanders, formerly of the Pittsburgh Steelers, to take his place.

After the free agency dust had settled, it was time for interviews.

When asked by the *Denver Post*'s Mike Klis, Fox said he would do everything differently in the lead up to the Super Bowl; a subtle testimony that the team is constantly competing for a Super Bowl win, and that the coach plans on getting back there soon.

Fox admitted he'd do, "Probably everything," differently. "Right now I'd like to get there," Fox said. "But even my kids were getting on me: Getaway hotel, dad, that's 80 percent bad."

A day earlier, John Elway clarified the franchise's goal.

"We're chasing Lombardi," he told media members during the NFL Owner's Meetings in late March, 2014. Classic Elway. All or nothing.

"Mentality-wise on defense we got better," Elway told Klis. "Talib will bring that mentality. Ware brings some mentality. T.J. Ward is a physical guy. Not that we didn't have it before, but we had a lot of guys injured, too.

"And I think where we need that mentality, too, is we have to step up there on offense, too."

In April, Manning again spoke to Mike Klis of the *Denver Post* about his forward-looking philosophy.

"You have to move forward," Manning said. "You have to kind of re-establish your identity of the 2014 team. The 2013 team—it was a good season in a lot of ways. There is no question it did not end the way we wanted it to, but we have to find a way to build off that and take a step further. Try to finish.

"There is no question you have to kind of start over again and re-establish the chemistry on this team with all these new players. I think that's important, and that really starts on Monday."

Chemistry is underrated, there's no doubt it improved in 2013 with players like Demaryius Thomas, Eric Decker and Knowshon Moreno. But, Decker and Moreno departed for greener pastures and greener jerseys—Decker with the New York Jets and Moreno with the Miami Dolphins—meaning the opportunity to bond as new teammates has presented itself once again.

"We lost many players and some great friends," Manning explained. "That's the worst part about football. When you form some friendships with these guys and really put a lot of hard work in—the business side comes into play. We added some great players. I'm excited about working with them starting on Monday." That week, the team began organized offseason workouts.

The NFL Draft was in early May. Usually the event is in April; this was the first Draft ever held in May, as the league year was moved back two weeks in 2014.

Two things can be said about John Elway's Drafts; the team tends to be less aggressive than in free agency, and no one truly knows what the team will do because he keeps his cards close to his chest.

This time around, Elway's fourth as the leader of the front office, the Broncos made some bold decisions.

First and foremost, they didn't trade down and out of the first round like many believed they would, nor did they trade up; Denver took Bradley Roby at No. 31 overall. Roby is an incredibly fast cornerback with solid size and great ball-playing ability. The Broncos expect him to make an immediate impact, playing at the No. 2 cornerback role on passing downs with Chris Harris in the slot.

In the second round, the Broncos took a gamble. They moved up, from 63 to 56 in a trade with the San Francisco 49ers, taking Cody Latimer out of Indiana. Latimer is a tall receiver who has much room to grow according to draft scouts and his highlight reels. He must learn how to run more precise routes—especially with Manning at quarterback—and needs to be more physical. One factor making this a questionable decision is that he was drafted with a broken foot; arguably the worst kind of injury for a player relying on speed and running a ton. What's more is some scouts rated him as a fourth or fifth round player, while Denver moved up into the mid-late second to take him. San Francisco traded back into 57, basically stealing the Broncos' fourth round pick of the 2014 draft, only to almost kick sand in Denver's faces.

In the third round, Denver took offensive tackle Michael Schofield to add depth to the line, and center Matt Paradis in the fifth round will help in that department, as well. In the fifth and seventh rounds, the Broncos found two linebackers in Lamin Barrow and Corey Nelson.

Of course, it's much too soon to grade the Broncos 2014 Draft. The team is still getting returns back to 2009 and Elway's first, 2011; Nate Irving has the opportunity in 2014 to become the fifth starter from that draft, which would make it an exceptional victory.

In late May, more Broncos legal troubles arose.

One was connected to the previous summer. Matt Russell was sentenced for his crimes which were outlined in Chapter 3. Newcomer T.J. Ward also found himself on the hot-seat.

On May 22, news broke regarding Ward and an arrest warrant which had been issued. On May 23, Ward appeared in court facing disturbing-the-peace and misdemeanor assault charges; a court date was set for June

23. Ward allegedly had a late night altercation wherein he threw a glass mug at a bartender; the Broncos wanted toughness, this wasn't what they were looking for.

Russell's sentencing came May 23. A Colorado court decided on seven months of jail time, along with two years of monitored probation for charges stemming from rear-ending a State Trooper in July.

It was the fourth time a Broncos player or executive—Tom Heckert and Von Miller—were in legal trouble in under a year; a disturbing trend. It was a bad look for the Broncos organization, long known for demanding classier standards from all who represent it.

As those problems were addressed, Peyton Manning was busy giving a commencement speech at the University of Georgia. Manning's intelligence and his charm were on display that day, making the graduates laugh when retelling stories of dating his wife, a Georgia alumnus, saying she couldn't get into his alma mater, Tennessee. He, of course, threw passes to some new alumni and gave some sage advice.

When the team met for mandatory mini-camp in June, they received their AFC Championship rings. Manning had something to say about them, about their 2013 season and the one which was rapidly approaching.

"We did a lot of good things last year and we need to build on those things -- you just don't go out and go a step further because you went that far last year," Manning explained. "It's 'Why did we get that far last year?' It's because we put a lot of hard work in and we had a great offseason and a great training camp. We're off to a start that way as well but we have to go out and do it again and then try to find a way to finish it. That's what the meeting was about last night and I thought Coach Fox was very clear on what the goals were, what the goals are for this season."

The Broncos learned who they would be playing in 2014 and it all sets up for some gritty matchups on the gridiron.

The Broncos had a relatively weak schedule in 2013, exploiting some mediocre and even bad teams. It doesn't appear to be that way in 2014. Denver is set to play the NFC West, regarded as the best, most physical division in all of football. The Seahawks and San Francisco 49ers are typical of that toughness, while the Arizona Cardinals and even St. Louis Rams—with their top-notch pass-rush—have improved as of late.

Week 3 is the game everyone will be waiting for. The Broncos start their season with two home games—Manning hosts the Colts, followed by the Chiefs—before Denver flies to Seattle to face the Seahawks for the first time since the Super beat down. Their bye follows, in week 4. It comes early for the Broncos this season, who are used to it coming in the middle of their season slate.

Week 7, hosting the 49ers will be a tough test. Then it's Brady–Manning XVI in Foxborough for Week 9. Week 13 at the Chiefs could decide the AFC West and a road game against the Bengals will be difficult in the second to last week.

Without a doubt, the Denver Broncos are one of the most successful organizations in the NFL, that prosperity has been renewed in recent years with the Duke of Denver calling the shots.

In 2011, Elway emerged as the new leader of the Broncos, hired John Fox, who gave Tim Tebow a shot. When the fans called for Tebow, they got him, and everyone connected to the organization went on the ride of a lifetime. Fans also asked for the team to go back to predominantly orange jerseys; they were granted that wish as well. 2011 surely won't go down as a triumphant season—finishing 8-8, backing into the playoffs only to beat the Pittsburgh Steelers—but it started the upward trend, doubling the previous season's win total and garnering a post-season victory.

2012 went better than anyone could have expected; 13-3 with the No. 1 seed in Manning's first year back to the gridiron, his first year with the Broncos. But once the team got to that point, they became the favorites, which is why the "Fail Mary" was so shocking and disturbing to Denver fans.

2013 seemed to be the year of Denver's destiny; they had enough talent to blow teams out with their explosive, NFL record-setting offense, but a rash of injuries and lack of toughness meant the Broncos demise.

The organization is rewarding its fans; not only have they listened to fans' desires, they consistently field a competitive football team, year in, year out.

The Broncos are set up as one of the most talented teams in the league for the 2014 season. While much has been made about the difficulty Denver will have in making it back to the Super Bowl—the 1972 Miami Dolphins were the last to lose and then become champions the next year—the Broncos are set up for yet another Super Bowl run. With Elway in charge and his declaration of "We're chasing Lombardi," the Broncos are in sure, capable, Super Bowl-winning hands; the future is nothing but bright in the Mile High City.

And that may mean we see a brilliant sunset on the Elway-Manning Era.

Stay tuned.

There's still much to be decided in the "Elway-Manning Era" as we put it here in the book, we recognize that and it's why there was a need for this "look ahead" chapter.

But, what can't be missed is the phenomenal work that's been done by John Elway, his front office cohorts and by Pat Bowlen by allowing them to spend the money necessary to compete.

Mission accomplished? That'd be as foolish as hanging a giant banner declaring victory.

No, Elway, Manning and the many, many men that make up the Denver Broncos are not satisfied, they're not complete, and they're not finished until they win a Super Bowl together. That much is clear, through Elway and Fox's speak, by Elway exclaiming, "We're chasing Lombardi" and by Fox constantly echoing those same sentiments.

Still, what's phenomenal is how far they've come, how far the team has come and in such a short time. From 4-12 to 13-3 in two years is almost unheard of, even in this wildly unpredictable, unstable, disparity-filled NFL.

Has too much credit been given to Peyton Manning? Simply, yes. For years, too much onus has been placed on quarterbacks' shoulders, no matter how broad they may be. In wins, quarterbacks take all the glory and they're the goat in the losses, too. While Manning was the first and most important player John Elway signed during this era, Elway's long list of impact players must be noted. Elway built a team, quickly and extraordinarily, around Manning at the twilight of the legend's career.

Still, the Broncos didn't just have one weak link in 2013, they had two. There are three phases to a football team; offense, defense and special teams. And, similarly to the way it was written here, we football fans think of the game. In 2014, offense comes first. Scoring points is important to us because, well, it's fun, it keeps our attention, and it's exciting. In this instant gratification society, we want scores, lots of them, and quickly. Denver was perfect for that, better than any team in the history of the league at keeping our attention, yet, they weren't the best team in football.

That's because the defense was deficient and special teams was a complete drain on the squad as a whole. Of course, injuries weakened both phases; but in the NFL, there's no room to make excuses. There is only time—a short amount of it at that—to make your team better. Which is, again, why John Elway must be commended for the work he's put in, the construction of a (AFC) championship team, and how he's attacked those deficiencies head on through the offseason.

The Broncos' 2013 offense was their best ever, but it's difficult to argue the 2012 team wasn't better, all-around. Not only was Manning and the offense awesome, but the dynamic duo of Von Miller and Elvis Dumervil caused quarterbacks to quake in their cleats and forced many turnovers. At the same time, Trindon Holliday was electric as a return man, hiding the mostly terrible play in that phase of the game.

In 2013, the lack of consistent pass-rush allowed quarterbacks to pick apart the secondary which was thrown together with newcomers (Dominique Rodgers-Cromartie), rookies (Kayvon Webster) and even an undrafted youngster (Duke Ihenacho) due to injuries.

On special teams, it was a matter of "when will they mess up?" in 2013, and as we saw in the book, it happened a lot. Almost every game in 2013, or at least in every one of the most important contests, was there a massive mistake by the special teams unit. Kickoff returns are being phased out of the NFL, and yet, Denver allowed huge return after huge return to set up opposing teams with amazing field position. It all doesn't calculate into winning football.

Still, the Broncos' booming offense hid those sad special teams and even made the defense an afterthought. They were dominant because of that offense, but it wasn't enough to win the Super Bowl; Elway's working on that.

As Vince Lombardi famously said, "Once you learn to quit, it becomes a habit." Elway has always been a winner, he persevered through three Super Bowl blowouts in the 1980s and became a champion himself in the late 90s by winning at all costs, literally giving up his body for the good of the team.

Now the Duke of Denver is making sure losing doesn't become a habit for this team because winning at all costs has always been Elway's calling card.

For Elway, much like Lombardi in the 1950s and 1960s, "Winning isn't everything, it's the only thing."

In that way, Elway and the Broncos are both chasing Lombardi's legend and also chasing the coveted trophy which bears his name.

REFERENCES

CH. 2

Kirwan, Pat, and David Seigerman. 2011. Take Your Eye off the Ball: How to Watch Football by Knowing Where to Look. Chicago: Triumph Books.

Badard, Greg. 2013. "Wes Welker leaves Patriots, Signs with Broncos." Boston Globe, March 13. http://www.boston.com/sports/football/patriots/2013/03/13/wes-welker-leaves-patriots-signs-with-broncos/kW5jYv6kx2iAIhRDIAGciK/story.html

CH. 4

Katzowitz, Josh. 2013. "Von Miller two hours late to court appearance; magistrate not pleased." CBSsports.com, October 28. http://www.cbssports.com/nfl/eye-on-football/24151348/von-miller-misses-court-appearance-magistrate-not-pleased

Maass, Brian. 2013. "Broncos' Von Miller Again Facing Legal Trouble." denver.cbslocal.com, September 10. http://denver.cbslocal.com/2013/09/10/von-miller-in-more-legal-trouble/

TheDenverChannel.com Team. 2013. "Denver Broncos linebacker Von Miller arrested on outstanding traffic warrant at Centennial Gun Club." TheDenverChannel.com, March 20. http://www. thedenverchannel.com/sports/broncos/denver-broncos-linebacker-von-miller-arrested-on-outstanding-traffic-warrant

CH. 7

Bell, Jarret. 2013. "Colts Jim Irsay: No Regrets Releasing Peyton Manning." USAToday.com, October 15. http://www.usatoday.com/story/sports/nfl/colts/2013/10/15/indianapolis-colts-jim-irsay-no-regrets-peyton-manning/2984615/

Klis, Mike. 2013. "John Fox fires back at Jim Irsay over Peyton Manning bashing." DenverPost.com, October 15. http://blogs. denverpost.com/broncos/2013/10/15/john-fox-fires-back-jim-irsay-peyton-manning-bashing/22496/

CH. 10

Jensen, Tom. 2014. "3rd Annual NFL Poll" Public Policy Polling, January 4. http://www.publicpolicypolling.com/main/2014/01/3rd-annual-nfl-poll.html

Layden, Tim. 2014. "There's a story behind Knowshon Moreno's tears." SI.com, January 8. Shttp://sportsillustrated.cnn.com/nfl/news/20140108/knowshon-moreno/

CH. 11

Jones, Lindsay H. 2013. "After Patriots divorce, Wes Welker at home with Broncos." USAToday.com, November 21. http://www.usatoday.com/story/sports/nfl/broncos/2013/11/21/wes-welker-tom-brady-denver-broncos-new-england-patriots/3669563/

Kensler, Tom. 2014. "Terranace Knighton gets key sack for Broncos in AFC Championship Game." DenverPost.com, January 19. http://www.denverpost.com/broncos/ci_24947509/terrance-knighton-gets-key-sack-broncos-afc-championship

CH. 12

Billick, Brian. 2011. "'Toxic differential' an essential indicator of success in NFL." NFL.com, November 17. http://www.nfl.com/news/story/09000d5d82435ffb/article/toxic-differential-an-essential-indicator-of-success-in-nfl

Klemko, Robert. 2014. "Richard Sherman refuses to go quietly into the night." MMQB.si.com, February 3. http://mmqb.si.com/2014/02/03/richard-sherman-super-bowl-48-seattle-seahawks/

CH. 13

Klis, Mike. 2014. "John Elway simplifies Broncos' goal for 2014: 'We're Chasing Lombardi." DenverPost.com, March 24. http://www.denverpost.com/broncos/ci_25409664/john-elway-simplifies-broncos-goal-2014-were-chasing

Klis, Mike. 2014. "John Fox would do 'everything' differently if Broncos return to Super Bowl." DenverPost.com, March 25. http://www.denverpost.com/broncos/ci_25414923/john-fox-would-do-everything-differently-if-broncos

Klis, Mike. 2014. "Peyton Manning looks forward to new season with new teammates." DenverPost.com, April 17. http://www.denverpost.com/broncos/ci_25582843/peyton-manning-looks-forward-new-season-new-teammates